A WORLD APART

To my wife Lynda

A WORLD APART

CREATING A CHURCH
FOR THE UNCHURCHED

Martin Robinson

MONARCH
Tunbridge Wells

British Library Cataloguing in Publication Data
A catalogue record for this book is available from
the British Library.

ISBN 1 85424 174 5 (Monarch)
ISBN 0 948704 37 3 (BCGA)

The BCGA acknowledges the financial assistance received from the Drummond
Trust, 3 Pitt Terrace, Stirling, in the co-publication of this book.

'This book is co-published with the Church Pastoral Aid Society, Athena Drive,
Tachbrook Park, Warwick CV34 6NG. CPAS is a mission agency which exists to
strengthen churches to evangelise, teach and pastor people of all ages. It seeks through
people and resources to stimulate evangelism, equip and train leaders, advice about
ministry and make grants for mission and training.'

This book is also co-published with the British Church Growth Association. For
details please see end of book.

Production and printing in England
for MONARCH PUBLICATIONS
Owl Lodge, Langton Road, Speldhurst, Kent TN3 0NP by
Nuprint Ltd, Station Road, Harpenden, Herts AL5 4SE.

Contents

Foreword

WILLOW CREEK COMMUNITY CHURCH is built on the biblical premise that people matter to God and, therefore, they should matter to us. Our goal is to live out this value by innovating new ways to express the age-old gospel message to secular people who are disinterested in God, the Bible and the church.

For us, this has meant using contemporary styles of music, modern forms of drama, and messages that are both true to God's Word and relevant to the lives of unchurched people. In short, we've tried to crack our own cultural code—to "become all things to all men"—for the purpose of effectively communicating a critically important message to segments of our society largely untouched by modern churches.

Our aim has always been to be a God-honouring church that worships Him, edifies believers, reaches the lost and extends tangible Christian love to those in physical and emotional need. Our purpose has never been to grow to any particular size or to start a new denomination. We simply want to be true to His calling to be a 20th century expression of a New Testament church.

But over the years an interesting development has occurred. First in our own country and then increasingly in other places around the world, church leaders began to look to Willow Creek for ideas and encouragement. They felt that by observing what God had led us to do and then applying a similar ministry approach in their own neighbourhoods, they could begin to crack their own cultural codes and become more effective in penetrating the secular strata of their societies with the gospel message. And so in this way the vision has spread.

Among church leaders in the U.K., Martin Robinson has been at the forefront of examining and scrutinizing the Willow Creek approach. In this book he presents an excellent overview of what's happening at our church and, more importantly, he offers an incisive analysis of the British church scene along with suggestions concerning Willow Creek ministry principles that might be transferable.

It is my hope that you will read this book with an open mind and prayerful heart, asking God to give you direction and courage to do whatever is necessary to value and reach lost people for Him. Let it inspire you to new levels of commitment to discovering new ways of penetrating the British culture with the life-changing and eternity-altering message of Jesus Christ.

Bill Hybels, Senior Pastor
Willow Creek Community Church
South Barrington, Illinois
May, 1992

Introduction

WILLOW CREEK COMMUNITY CHURCH is reputedly the fastest-growing protestant church in North America. It is said to be the second largest protestant church in the United States and could soon be the largest if its present growth continues. But the importance of Willow Creek, not just for North America but also for the continent of Europe, lies neither in its rapid growth nor in its size, but rather in its stated aim: to be a church that is consciously attempting to reach those in its community who are unchurched.

It is possible that the size of Willow Creek could lead to another misunderstanding. This book is not intended to be a book about how to run a large church, nor will it be argued that large churches are always a good thing. It is true that it often takes more resources, both in terms of money and people, to reach the unchurched than we realise; this is particularly true of large cities. So it may well be that it does require a large church to break through the many competing messages that a large city proclaims in such profusion. It is also the case that too often the church is guilty of thinking too small and of missing the potential of the large, or at least the larger, church. Nevertheless, this book is not really attempting to make a case for a particular size of church, if only because it will require a variety of sizes and styles of church to meet the very different challenges that each community brings. Not everyone lives in a large city and will feel well served by a large church.

The intention of this book is to explore what it means to reach the unchurched, those who share our world in so many respects but who in one important area live in a world apart from any knowledge of Christian faith and hope. The barrier that has grown up between those who attend church regularly and those who know nothing at all about the Christian faith has become so complete that it has become increasingly difficult for the church to communicate across this chasm of separation. The evangelistic strategies of most churches centre around attempts to reach the natural fringe of the church, and then to seek to expand that fringe. In short, they are directed to the world that is nearest to the church. This book does not seek to criticise such an evangelistic strategy but instead suggests that it is necessary to open a second front, one which will attempt to see the church planted in the very midst of those who live totally apart from the church.

The book is divided into three parts. The first part attempts to consider some of the historical causes that have produced a situation in which so many people have come to be alienated from the church, and to reflect a little on this process. Those who have a more practical than theoretical bias might find this first section rather hard work. If you do, you have my permission to proceed straight to part two! This looks in some detail at the particular story and approach of Willow Creek as it relates to its single-minded attempt to reach the unchurched.

Part three examines a variety of case histories of churches or projects located in Great Britain, all of which are attempting to reach different groups of unchurched people in their respective communities. In selecting these case histories, it was tempting to visit those 'success stories' of which I was aware, some of which are already well known. Instead, I have chosen situations which for the most part are not yet publicised to any great degree. Some of them are so new that their eventual outcome is by no means certain. They have been chosen not to provide examples to imitate but in the hope that they might inspire creative responses in those who consider and reflect on what they read.

Some attempt has been made, in selecting case histories, to offer a wide variety. This variety is reflected in the parts of the country in which they are located, in the varying groups of people that they are seeking to reach, in their denominational background and in the mix of newly planted churches as compared to situations which are attempting a transition from an older established church to one which seeks to have a somewhat sharper cutting edge in relation to the unchurched.

Part of the intention of dividing the book into these three rather different parts is the hope that such an approach will assist us in our attempt to look not just at models but at some of their underlying principles. I am convinced that the precise application of these principles at Willow Creek is necessarily culturally defined, and so cannot be transferred to different cultural situations. But the underlying principles are most certainly transferable. The expression of these principles in other contexts requires creativity and imagination. I hope that this book will contribute to a debate in which other forms of expression might be encouraged. Hopefully, those who read it will be stimulated to discover a whole range of imaginative solutions to the fundamental task of contacting, convincing and discipling the many thousands of individuals who at present stand completely outside of any of the churches that are currently in existence.

In Acts 11:19–21 we read the following words:

> Now those who had been scattered by the persecution in connection with Stephen travelled as far as Phoenicia, Cyprus and Antioch, telling the message only to Jews. Some of them, however, men from Cyprus and Cyrene, went to Antioch and began to speak to Greeks also, telling them the good news about the Lord Jesus. The Lord's hand was with them, and a great number of people believed and turned to the Lord.

How strange that we should not even know the names of those who were responsible for perhaps the greatest missionary breakthrough that the church has ever made, crossing the boundary between Jews and Greeks! It is no coincidence that Antioch was to become one of the greatest missionary churches of the early church. It was the sending church for Paul and Barnabas. No church that Paul and Barnabas planted was ever exactly the same as the church at Antioch; but the underlying principle, that inspiration to take the message to whoever would listen, came directly from their sending church. May we also have the courage to move from our familiar forms, so that any and all who may care to hear the gospel may do so in forms that are familiar and understandable to the world of which they are a part.

CHAPTER ONE

A *Hostile Environment For The Gospel*

THE SCENE WAS A WINDSWEPT, bleak, high-density council housing estate of the type built so optimistically in the 1960s. The wind funnelled through twin tower blocks creating a mini whirlwind, blowing piles of old newspapers and other rubbish into new shapes. Small packs of dogs padded along aimlessly, narrowly avoiding the wheels of cars on the main road. I was speaking to a man who was a leader in a small church which, against all the odds, had managed to remain despite the redevelopment of the area and was now struggling to keep its doors open.

'I joined this church in 1930,' he told me, 'and it's been in decline ever since.' I am sure that he was not making any causal connection between these two events, but his voice betrayed how his experience of decline had shaped his view of the potential for the gospel message.

Over the last five years, I have travelled more than 100,000 miles visiting churches in connection with my job as a Consultant to Bible Society. If that experience has taught me anything, it has brought home the amazing diversity of church life around the world. There are many experiences of decline, of hopelessness, of heroic efforts that have proved to be fruitless or even misguided.

Equally there are many churches that exude new life, confidence and renewal. I remember one woman who told me that she became a Christian in the 1950s, was still a member of the same church that she joined then, and had never had experience of a declining church. The church that she had first joined had simply grown steadily and healthily over the whole period of her Christian experience. Nevertheless, despite the variety, richness and sometimes surprising joy of church life in Britain, most Christians are aware that communicating the Christian faith to those outside the walls of Christian worship and fellowship is not easy in our land.

Yet the church around the world is growing as it has never grown before. The net growth of the church is estimated to be some 70,000 persons per day.[1] More impressive than the bare statistics is the fact that during this century the growth of the church has been greatest in those areas of the world where the Christian church has previously been numerically weak. Indeed, overall growth has been achieved despite the relative decline of the church in those parts of the world where it used to be strong.

In percentage terms, the size of the church has remained more or less constant during the twentieth century: 34% of the world's population. This figure has been maintained in the face of dramatic population growth in those parts of the world where the church was hardly represented 100 years ago. In other words, it would not have been possible to have maintained such a percentage figure without very large numbers of conversions in newly evangelized areas of the world.

Such figures stand in stark contrast to the expectations of some noted experts on population growth. In 1968 the International Review of Mission contained this forecast:

Towards the end of this century, Christians will comprise no more than eight per cent of the world's population— assuming that present demographic growth will not be arrested in some unforeseen manner.... Even the best missionary strategy with a conventional approach to the field of church planting and church growth will have no material effect upon this prognosis.[2]

The expert concerned was not being foolish. His demographic projections were absolutely accurate. Nor was he wrong to suggest that missionary strategies as such could hardly change the situation. What has happened was something entirely unforeseen. There has been an explosion in evangelistic activity on the part of Third-World Christians which has been so astonishingly successful that the seemingly inevitable projection that Christians would become only 8% of the world's population by the end of the century has actually been refuted by a percentage figure of 34% that is still rising!

But despite this relatively good news in terms of the global experience of Christianity, the experience of the church in Western Europe during the greater part of the twentieth century stands in marked contrast to the picture of growth and optimism elsewhere. Why should this be so? Why is it that the church in places like India and Nigeria should find it possible to think in terms of growth, whereas the church in countries such as Britain and France should have seen such relentless decline and pessimism?

Those who are familiar with the church in all of these countries do not believe that the Christians they meet in India are any more faithful or zealous for growth than those they meet in Bradford or Birmingham. Is there a problem with the methodology of the church in Europe compared to the church in other lands, or is there something about the context in which the European church finds itself that somehow acts against its potential growth?

THE ALIENATION OF THE CHURCH

There are many in the church today who yearn passionately for the West to become significantly more committed to the Christian faith which has played such an important part in shaping Western culture and history. In such circumstances, it is all too tempting to imagine that there was once a golden age when all men and women in Christendom were devout, believing Christians. Such a notion is almost certainly a romantic illusion. That the Christian faith once held a place of prominence in the life of Western nations is without doubt. That the thoughts and aspirations of some of our greatest thinkers were inspired by the Christian faith is also not disputed. That the parish church represented the centre of community life throughout a predominately rural society need not be questioned. But the quality of understanding and spirituality, and the extent to which a vital and informed Christian faith penetrated all sections of society, is very much a matter of debate. It does not take much reading of English national literature, whether Chaucer's Canterbury Tales or the poetry of John Donne, to see that the quality of Christian commitment has varied a great deal over the centuries.

True, there have been times of great spiritual renewal that spread through all of Western Europe; the great reform movement of the late eighth and early ninth centuries inspired by Bishop Chrodegang of Metz, the reform movement of the late tenth and early eleventh centuries produced by Cluny in Burgandy, the great monastic revivals of the twelfth century and of course the reform movement that we know better as the Reformation, beginning in the sixteenth century–these, and other events in the life of the church, burned deep into the national consciousness, and as they did so helped to form many of the institutions which today we take for granted as part of our national life. But as for the actual beliefs and spirituality of the ordinary working person, the extant literature suggests that there was often a mixture of pagan ideas, folk superstition and simple nature worship worked into the general Christian framework for faith that was available.

Nor should those of us who stand in the Protestant tradition too easily accept our own propaganda and believe that such apparent ignorance was caused by the witholding of the Bible from ordinary people because of a conspiracy of priests. Far from improving after the Reformation when the Bible was more generally available to ordinary people, the position if anything worsened. By the early eighteenth century when the effect of the Reformation on British church life was so well established as to be virtually irreversible, the Christian faith was at a low ebb indeed. The 'Age of Reason', as the early eighteenth century is known, produced a theology known as deism which was really a form of natural religion. Deism looked to the created world rather than to the historical faith of the Bible for its religious inspiration. Gerald Cragg describes the impact of such religion in this way: 'The age of reason had forgotten certain fundamental human needs; natural religion might satisfy the minds of some, but the hearts of the multitudes were hungry.'[3]

Those who live in the United States often look back to the origins of their own nation and recall that it was a nation that was founded on a strong belief in God. However, it is all too often forgotten that the kind of faith that prevailed at the time of the Declaration of Independence was not necessarily a strong evangelical faith but resembled much more closely the fashionable deism of the age. During this period in Britain, the Church of England had become strongly identified with the ruling squirearchy, so much so that by the middle of the century it was not equipped 'to meet the religious needs of the fast rising urban population, especially in the industrial towns of the north where parishes were large and churches few, and suffered increasing pastoral neglect.'[4]

Nor were the Nonconformist churches in a position to fill the gap left by the inadequacies of the Anglican church. They had been the losers in the Settlement following the turbulent years of the Commonwealth period. Their churches were allowed to operate on a very restricted basis and their members had become introverted, placing their emphasis on a kind of pietism that allowed them to survive but not to grow. By the middle of the century they were estimated to form no more than 2.5% of the total population. Catholicism survived during this time as an illegal church, particularly in the North-West of England and in parts of Scotland; but it too was concerned with survival and could not even think of expansion.

Had this remained the situation of the whole church in

England, then it would have been ill-equipped indeed to cope with the vast changes that were about to overtake British society as the impact of the agricultural and industrial revolutions produced in Britain the first predominately industrial— and so urban—society that the world had ever known. Robin Gamble, in a recent work on the response of the church to such a situation, eloquently describes the effect of such changes: 'The results were at once gloriously uplifting and witheringly degrading. For a few it meant fabulous wealth, but for many it meant the crushing of hope and the ending of dignity.'[5]

Fortunately, just a few short years before the full impact of the industrial revolution had been unleashed on British society, there had emerged a movement of great spiritual vigour which although it owed much to the efforts of many devoted men and women of God is often known today as the Wesleyan revival. The evangelical movement, of which the Wesleys were only really a part, was to have an influence on all aspects of the church, even on those parts of it which did not share its theology and experience.

The impact of the evangelical revival went beyond those who were part of its immediate membership. Clearly the power of the revival meant that it was able to shape the religious and social landscape of the nineteenth century, both in terms of specific social reforms and in helping to set a broader agenda for values in society. One writer describes this influence as follows:

> Moreover, undergirding all the official forms of Christianity were increasingly rigorous public standards of moral behaviour and Sabbath observance, and a renewed attention to private Bible-reading and daily family prayer.[6]

Although it can be strongly argued that the evangelical revival actually began in the Church of England, it was the Nonconformists who first felt the greatest impact of the revival, beginning in the last part of the eighteenth century but continuing strongly throughout the first half of the nineteenth century. The flexible structures of the Nonconformist churches allowed them to capitalise on the huge growth that took place in the cities. Robin Gamble documents their initiative very well:

> The first half of the nineteenth century was a time of explosive growth for the Nonconformists. They were developing work in the industrial areas years before Anglicanism woke up to the new facts of life. For example, Dukinfield in Lancashire had built up a population of 10,000 before an Anglican church was built in 1848, by which time there were seventeen chapels in the town. In the West Riding licenses issued for new nonconformist places of worship increased from seventy-three in the 1780s to 401 in the 1790s. In this period the Methodists saw their membership increase ninefold, the Independent Congregationalists increased sixfold, whilst the Baptists saw a sevenfold increase.[7]

By the middle of the nineteenth century the Church of England, aided partly by earlier reforms and possibly spurred on by the realisation that the gains of Nonconformity had severely challenged its position as the national church, was engaged with some degree of success in a conscious attempt to respond to the demands of Victorian England. The Roman Catholic church, now able to operate legally and considerably larger as a result of Irish immigration, was also playing its part in the religious life of the great cities of Britain. But the apparent vigour of religious life in nineteenth-century Britain was to some extent misleading; not because it was not genuine, but much more because it was confined to certain segments of society.

Anglicanism had become identified with the upper classes and with that small part of the working classes that might be called the deferential working class. Roman Catholicism, which had previously depended so heavily on the loyalty of a few aristocratic families, was now strongly identified with the Irish immigrant subculture within Britain. The Nonconformist churches, many of which had started with working-class roots, had become strongly identified with the new middle classes and at best with that part of the working class which aspired to self-improvement.

Moreover, many Nonconformist churches had become caught in a kind of cultural captivity, whereby the particular expression of the faith that each church or chapel espoused had become so identified with the life of particular communities that it was almost impossible for that form of faith to move outside its chosen community. Worse still, if the community itself were to change its culture it would be almost impossible for the chapel to change without seeming to lose the very values that had made it so successful in the first place. Successful adaptation to the needs of particular communities had caused the churches to become cultural islands, increasingly cut off by the flowing river of change.

The great majority of the burgeoning working classes stood outside all this religious fervour. Certainly there were some working-class people in movements such as the Primitive Methodists with their preachers, popularly known as 'ranters'. Others, for example the Salvation Army, the preaching of individuals such as Gipsy Smith, the organised crusades of visitors such as Dwight Moody, all attempted to reach out to the alienated working classes; but somehow all of this activity did not succeed in capturing the heart of working people.

Those same working people, who when living in the countryside had not necessarily had deeply-formed Christian convictions, had discovered that their move to the city meant above all, a desperate struggle for survival and at best some simple relief from the drabness and misery that lay all around. The pub was more likely to provide such a haven than was the book-orientated worship of Victorian Protestantism. One contemporary commentator on the religious condition of working people noted:

> More especially in cities and large towns it is observable how absolutely insignificant a portion of the congregations is composed of artisans. They fill, perhaps, in youth, our

National, British, and Sunday Schools, and there receive the elements of a religious education; but, no sooner do they mingle in the active world of labour than, subjected to the constant action of opposing influences, they soon become utter strangers to religious ordinances as the people of a heathen country.[8]

Serious as this general failure to reach the hearts and minds of working people was, a much more significant challenge was beginning to emerge as the nineteenth century ended and the twentieth century began.

THE SPREAD OF SECULARISM

The decline of church attendance during the greater part of the twentieth century has been apparent for all to see. It was a decline that affected virtually all Protestant churches from 1918 onwards but more obviously impacted Nonconformist churches than any other segment of church life. All observers are agreed on the dramatic nature of nonconformity's decline, but few can agree on why it took place. James Munson commented that at the end of the nineteenth century nonconformity 'had all the attributes of power: it was vibrant, self confident and arrogant.' Yet, as Munson continues:

By 1919 it seemed to many then, and to more later, dated and something of a relic. Since then it has declined as a power in the land and its members have shrunk as a proportion of the population. How could a force which had been so influential in English life for so long and which, by the end of the nineteenth century, was so powerful decline so quickly in the decades after 1919?[9]

The mistake of many observers is to look too closely at nonconformity as if it was a sole casualty of what was taking place. Certainly it was the first and most obvious victim of a process that has come to affect nearly all expressions of mainstream church life in Britain. There are particular reasons why nonconformity was more open to the erosion of its numbers, and why the Anglican and Roman Catholic churches held out for longer; but by the end of the twentieth century it has become clear that all religious communities are affected by an underlying cause of decline. Indeed at this point in the twentieth century there is some evidence to suggest that nonconformity, albeit in dramatically new cultural clothes, is now growing slightly again and that while the Anglican church remains somewhat static in terms of its numerical strength, it is the Roman Catholic church that is now suffering the greatest decline in attendance of any of the major churches.[10]

The process to which we refer, and which has represented the underlying cause of decline in religious commitment in Europe as a whole, is that of the gradual secularisation of society. Strangely, the origins of secularism do not lie in the twentieth century or even in the nineteenth century but even earlier in what we have already referred to as the Age of Reason, sometimes known as the Enlightenment. The twin emphases of the Enlightenment were the theories of empiricism, which became the basis of modern scientific method, and of rationalism, which became the basis of modern philosophy. Ironically the majority of the early exponents of both strands of the movement which came to be known as the Enlightenment were devout Christians who could hardly have imagined the time bomb which was waiting to explode centuries later.

There is no space in this book to explore the precise process by which secular thought has come to occupy such a place of prominence in our public life. Others, notably Lesslie Newbigin, have performed this service very well indeed.[11] However, we do need to be aware that the most critical effect of secularism has been to cause our culture to make a distinction between the public world of facts and the private world of opinion. In such a framework, the world of science is held to be part of the world of facts and hence is presented as objective public truth, sufficiently trustworthy for our society to base its judgements and values on.

That same framework holds that religious faith, by contrast, belongs to the private world of opinion. Religious convictions may or may not be true, but in the final analysis they cannot be proved either way. Secularism asserts that in such a scenario, all faiths are equally valid provided that they remain firmly in the private sphere. By definition, as long as faith remains a private matter it cannot influence the public world. Faith, therefore, cannot act as a basis for the values, morals and judgements of society, only as the basis for an individual's private lifestyle. The further implied judgement is that religion is not only private and esoteric, but is essentially for those who are weak and easily exploited.

Newbigin and others have pointed out that the assertions of a scientific world view are far from being neutral, value-free statements. Rather, they involve some very profound faith convictions. In the face of such criticism, science often responds, 'Yes, but what we assert works. It offers a plausible, reasonable explanation of the way in which our world operates.'

Here we come to the heart of the matter. There can be little doubt that in many important respects, scientific method does offer a powerful means of understanding and even of subduing the world in which we live. But this is not quite the same thing as saying that science is able to offer a complete and satisfactory explanation of reality. What science does do is offer a very plausible response to the question 'How' things have happened; but it has very little to say in response to the question 'Why' they have happened.

However, we need to remember that in our very pragmatic culture, many have concluded that the question 'How do things happen?' is much more valid than the question 'Why do things happen?'. At a personal level such questions become 'Does it work?', as opposed to 'Is it true?' In short, at this time in our history, science offers a set of explanations, or world view, which seems to be much more plausible than any world view offered by religious faith.

The effect of the utter dominance of a scientific world view is often to produce one of two responses to religious assertions. The first is to be utterly incredulous that anyone at all can believe that there is an unseen God who responds to our prayers and who demands a moral response from us. The other response, even from those who can conceive of God as at least some 'higher power', is to respond to the Christian evangelist: 'Even if all you say about Jesus Christ is true, and even if he was raised from the dead—so what?'. It is this 'so what' response to which Christians are often unable to reply, and which has proved to be so damaging to organised religion.

THE COMING POST-SECULAR MAN

However, despite the fact that the dominant ideology of our day depends heavily on a secular, scientific world view, there is very little evidence to suggest that European man is becoming less religious. If anything, there seem to be strong indications of a new religious quest, though one which for the most part is not looking to Christianity for answers. Certainly a number of sects and cults related to Christianity have achieved some relatively significant growth in recent years. For example, Jehovah's Witnesses in Britain have grown from 61,913 in 1970 to 114,000 in 1990 and continue to experience strong growth.[12] What single Christian denomination could make a similar claim? But such groups tend to operate at the margins of our society and are not really likely to play any major part in the development of any new spiritual direction in our culture.

How then can we describe this new religious quest? At one level, it is nothing more than a deeply-buried religious ache. Roger Edrington was a minister in a working-class suburb of Birmingham during the late 1970s and early 1980s. He had come from America and had already had a fruitful evangelistic ministry in an urban priority area in Coventry. He was deeply concerned to understand the beliefs of those who said with some passion that they had no belief in God. As part of his quest for understanding, he undertook Ph.D. research with the thesis title, *The Mind of the Unbeliever*.[13] His method was to interview fifty working-class men over a two-year period.

The results of this research were deeply moving. After trust had been gained, it became apparent that nearly all of the men had prayed during their adult 'unbelieving' lives. Many could point to specific answers to prayer, some of which had made a deep impression on their lives. All were reluctant to admit to such experiences, apparently not because they were too personal but because the interviewees were deeply embarrassed at having had such experiences. It was as if religious faith and its accompanying experiences were simply not options for them. Somehow, the power of a scientific world view which excluded God was so much a part of their understanding of how they fitted into the order of things, that to have any religious feeling at all was to admit to being weak and consequently in need of an emotional crutch. Religious faith was associated with childhood, with the emotionally crippled, the mentally unstable or with those who were in it for some personal gain and hence were essentially hypocrites.

Yet strangely, as we have already commented, most if not all of these men had encountered moments of profound religious experience; and it is here that there lies a situation of genuine pathos. On the one hand, the actual, existential encounter of these men with the world was that of genuine religious experience; but on the other hand, their rational world view was such that all religious experience had to be denied.

Those who have worked in similar communities will know how strongly the research of Roger Edrington rings true, and what terrible hopelessness seems to follow. The consequence for many thousands of men and women has been to produce a terrible tearing of the psyche as if the very souls of men and women are being ripped apart. Who knows what dark and terrible forces may enter into the chasm created by such fundamental tensions? There is increasing evidence in our society of the appalling consequences of such spiritual torpor. All too often, for example, sexual encounter acts as a substitute for spiritual encounter; and sexuality without spirituality carries with it a potential for disaster.

If the situation of those who dare not express belief represents the experience of many, particularly in working-class communities, there are many others who have become dissatisfied with such a state of affairs and have begun to experiment in a number of directions. I would suggest that we can think of such experimentation in three broad categories.

1. The search for other faiths

The arrival in Europe of significant communities of people of other faiths, together with a far greater awareness of other cultures in our world, through the media and travel, has helped to make the exploration of other faiths a much more realistic possibility for many Europeans. Buddhism is sometimes described as the fastest-growing religion in Britain. While such rapid growth is actually very small growth, starting as it does from a very small base, nevertheless a very high proportion of the total Buddhist community does consist of British converts many of whom occupy prominent positions in British national life. 12,000 people attended Buddhist retreats in Britain in 1983.[14]

It is much more difficult to document British converts to the various Hindu sects that exist in Britain; any converts are certainly vastly outnumbered by the large immigrant Hindu community from the sub-continent of India. But there are such converts and some of them have relatively high profiles, especially in such areas as the entertainment world. Islam claims to have made some 20,000 British converts; although possibly at least half of these are British women who have married Muslim men and for whom Islam means very little in terms of being a living faith, nevertheless there have also been some high-profile converts to Islam.

In addition to the variant forms of the ancient world faiths in Britain, there are also a number of 'newer' religions, many of which have come to the shores of Britain from the sunnier skies of California. Such groups often attract immediate followings which are often not maintained. However, government statistics suggest that as many as one million British people have at one time or another been involved with one or other of the faiths that have come to Britain in recent times, whether as missionary forms of the more ancient world religions or as representatives of the 'newer' religions.

It is true that significant numbers of Hindus, Sikhs, Muslims, Buddhists and those who have experimented with other religions have also converted to Christianity. The point of this discussion is not to demonstrate the relative strengths of one group or another so much as to note that such numbers indicate a surprisingly high level of religious search in an apparently secular society.[15]

2. The overtly occult

It is very hard to untangle myth from fact in this area. Those who claim to be involved in witchcraft, or wicca as it is now sometimes called, suggest that there are at least 100,000 people involved in regular coven worship. David Burnett offers the following estimate of the numerical strength of witchcraft:

> In 1989, the Occult Census reported 'a conservative estimated population of 250,000 Witches/Pagans throughout the UK and many more hundreds of thousands of people with a serious interest in Astrology, Alternative Healing Techniques and Psychic Powers.' These figures would appear to be somewhat inflated from the observation of the various resources that would indicate a lower figure of no more than 100,000, but having many fringe members.[16]

While it is almost impossible to be certain about such figures, few seasoned observers of the occult scene would seem to have grounds for disagreeing with this estimate. If the book trade is to be believed, literature on the occult sells well; and other indicators, such as the attention of the media and the experience of clergy in the rise in requests for exorcism, also suggest that the level of involvement is not inconsiderable. The rise of occult activity is not confined to the British Isles. Evidence from across Western Europe suggests that much the same pattern of resurgence can be detected elsewhere. It is frequently claimed that there are more mediums than priests in Paris and there seems no reason to believe that the growth of occult activity has reached anything like its peak.[17]

3. New Age activity

In more recent years we have seen the emergence of a combination of Eastern religions and occult practices which has been described as the New Age movement. The bewildering variety of manifestations of New Age activities which have developed as a consequence of such a fusion makes the New Age movement very difficult to categorise and describe. A recent publication from the Evangelical Alliance that seeks to explain New Ageism includes these words:

> The New Age roots are in a broad range of concepts, from evolutionary optimism and spiritism, to karma and reincarnation. From eastern pantheistic mysticism and science fiction to the Human Potential movement. Astrology and occult practices rub shoulders with the Green movement and alternative medicine.[18]

Just as it is difficult to describe the New Age movement, it is also hard to know exactly how many people are involved directly in its activities or are influenced by its philosophical and religious claims. What we do know is that hundreds of thousands of ordinary people visit the various psychic fairs which are held from time to time in major exhibition centres around the United Kingdom. The Glastonbury festival, with an estimated attendance of some 100,000, is an overt celebration of New Age philosophy.

The ideas which are popularised directly by New Age thinking find an unlikely ally in the very secularism which in its original form claims to reject all religious thought. Because secular thought makes the claim that all religious expression is a purely private matter and that all religious ideas are therefore as valid as each other, secularism acts to legitimise whatever religious ideas people care to formulate. Discussion in the public sphere of the objective value or otherwise of religious ideas becomes almost impossible in the framework of secularism.

Thus secular thought provides a protective shield for the emergence of any religious idea no matter how dangerous or bizarre it might be; while at the same time, because the dominance of a scientific or secular world view fails to satisfy the deepest religious longings of the human spirit, it actually makes inevitable the emergence of all kinds of religious ideology. What results for post-secular man is what we can only call a new paganism. No less an authority than the experienced missionary Lesslie Newbigin, commenting on some prophetic words of W.E. Gladstone written some 150 years ago, describes the society produced by the European Enlightenment as follows:

> What we have is, as Gladstone foretold, a pagan society whose public life is ruled by beliefs which are false. And because it is not a pre-Christian paganism, but a paganism born out of the rejection of Christianity, it is far tougher and more resistant to the gospel than the pre-Christian paganisms with which foreign missionaries have been in contact during the past 200 years. Here, without the possibility of question, is the most challenging missionary frontier of our time.[19]

FOOTNOTES

1. *A.D. 2000 Global Monitor* no 13 (Nov. 1991): p 2. Calculations based on figures given on this page.

2. *International Review of Mission* (July 1968): p 275.

3. Gerald R. Cragg, *The Church and the Age of Reason 1648-1789* (Pelican History of the Church vol 4: rev edn 1970), p 141.

4. Sheridan Gilley ed T. Thomas, *The British, Their Religious Beliefs and Practices 1800-1986* (Routledge: 1988), p 20.

5. Robin Gamble, *The Irrelevant Church* (Monarch: 1991), p 20.

6. Sheridan Gilley, *op cit*, p 21.

7. *Ibid*, p 29.

8. James Moore (ed), *Religion in Victorian Britain, Volume III Sources* (Manchester University Press: 1988), p 315.

9. James Munson, *The Nonconformists* (SPCK: 1991), p 291.

10. Figures in the latest MARC Europe Census project a continuing decline for Anglican and Roman Catholic church attendance through the 1990s. However the returns from the parishes are not quite so pessimistic and suggest that while the Roman Catholic church may well continue to experience decline, the Anglican figures may be more encouraging than the MARC figures suggest.

11. The work of Lesslie Newbigin has been developed through a project, initially funded by the British Council of Churches under the title, 'The Gospel and Our Culture' and based at Selly Oak Colleges in Birmingham. The project was inspired partly by a book written by Lesslie Newbigin, *The Other Side of 1984* (The Risk Book Series, WCC: 1983), and among its first publications is Hugh Montefiore (ed), *The Gospel and Contemporary Culture* (Mowbray: 1991).

12. For source see *A Century of Christianity: Historical Statistics 1900-1985 with projections to 2000* (MARC Monograph no 14, MARC Europe: 1989).

13. Roger Edrington's research was originally for a Ph.D. at Birmingham University and has since been published as Roger Edrington, *Everyday Men: Living in a Climate of Unbelief* (Lang: 1987).

14. Figure taken from a chapter by Deirdre Green, 'Buddhism in Britain: Skilful means or selling out?', to be found in: Paul Badham (ed), *Religion, State, and Society in Modern Britain* (Edwin Mellen: 1989), p 277.

15. The claim is made by E. Barker in the book *New Religious Movements: a Practical Introduction* (HMSO: 1989), that as many as 1,000,000 people in Britain have been members at one time or another of a 'New Religious Movement'.

16. David Burnett, *Dawning of the Pagan Moon* (Monarch: 1991), p 200.

17. A report in *The Times* offers evidence that witchcraft attracts more allegiance than the Roman Catholic church: 'Magic steals march on religion in Italy', *The Times* (6 January 1992).

18. 'New Age Promise, Age Old Problem?', *Past Present Future* (Evangelical Alliance: 1990), p 4.

19. Lesslie Newbigin, 'Can the West be Converted?', *Bulletin of Missionary Research* vol xi no 1 (January 1987): p 367.

CHAPTER TWO

Secularisation and the Contemporary Church

WRITERS SUCH AS LESSLIE NEWBIGIN have helped us to see that the issue of secularisation has impacted the church in every Western country. In addition, because of the influence of Western missions, the question of secularisation has also come to play a part in the experience of the church in other parts of the world. Yet the response of the contemporary church to this issue has seemed, superficially at least, to vary considerably in different countries. Let me illustrate these apparent differences by means of two personal stories.

It was two weeks before Christmas and the snow was two feet deep. The temperature was minus ten degrees fahrenheit with the wind-chill factor added. The snow was fine and powdered, the type that seems to be able to find its way into the tightest of boots. It was Tuesday evening: my partner and I were engaged in evangelistic visiting in the suburbs of Indianapolis. We scrambled across a snow drift to try to locate the exact house number that we wanted. I was grateful for at least two things—the block number system used by all American cities, which allowed me to find houses in the dark, and the local legislation that meant that all American householders had to clear the snow from the sidewalk immediately in front of their house.

Not a very promising occasion for evangelistic visiting, you
might think. Far from it. Once we had found the house and
rung the bell we received a very warm welcome indeed.
Around a dozen of us went on such calls every Tuesday
evening and we almost always received a ready response. But
evangelistic visiting Indianapolis-style was not quite the same
thing as it had been in inner-city Birmingham, England, which
had been the location of my previous church.

The people that we were calling on had all been first-time
visitors at last Sunday's worship service. Occasionally, if the
numbers in the evangelistic team were high and the number of
first-time visitors on the previous Sunday was low, then we
might receive a name from a list of people who had a slightly
more tenuous link with the church. But even on these calls, we
generally received a good welcome and were sometimes able to
lead people to a commitment to Christ. Positive responses to
this type of visiting were much more frequent than I had ever
known in calling on people's homes in Great Britain.

Some years later, as I told my story to an American minister
working in Britain, he gave me his definition of evangelism in
the American Mid-West. He said that it consisted of challenging people to do what they already knew they ought to do
anyway. My later travels in the United States told me, however, that there was not always a ready response to such an
appeal. Quite the opposite: on the Eastern seaboard, in the
North-West, in California and even in many of the larger cities
in the Mid-West itself, one was very likely to meet people who
were avowedly pagan and proud of it! The ready response of
people in the rural Mid-West seemed to be part of another
culture, another country, even of another world.

A short time after my return to the United Kingdom, I was
due to preach in a church in the North of England. I did not
expect to experience culture shock in my own land! The
chapel was in the middle of a long line of terraced houses—hard
to find if you didn't know exactly where it was. Its roof-height
was identical to that of the neighbouring houses. The chapel
shared a common gutter with one of the adjoining houses,

which produced arguments whenever the roof leaked as to who was responsible for the maintenance.

The main chapel door seemed to be locked but through the door of the schoolroom, left very slightly ajar, wafted the sounds of busy ladies preparing tea. I entered, for the moment unannounced and unnoticed. As I did so, I was able to take in a sight that I had seen many times before. Yet somehow this particular afternoon its familiarity struck me as both strange and depressing.

The walls of the schoolroom were painted with a dark green gloss to a height of some three feet above the floor. (No metric rule had ever entered here!) Above that came a black line not quite an inch wide. From there, the rest of the wall, right up to the simple plaster coving, was covered in a cream gloss paint. That was the Sunday School room. Here, generations of children had sung

> Hear the pennies dropping,
> Listen as they fall—
> Everyone for Jesus,
> He shall have them all,

as the offering was taken up. Had they, like me, wondered what Jesus did with all those ship halfpennies, or even how the ever-resourceful Sunday School Superintendent had conveyed them to Jesus?

Those cream walls had once been covered with posters of African and Indian children all seated round the feet of an Anglo-Saxon Jesus, a Jesus who had familiar blonde hair and beard and piercing blue eyes. This was long before the process of immigration had brought actual black and brown children to live in the streets around the chapel itself.

What happy days these walls had witnessed! Sunday School anniversaries had filled the place to capacity. Christmas parties and pantomines had produced squeal upon squeal of excitement. Summer Sunday School outings had been a highlight of the year, the only sight of the sea that many of those who went were ever likely to experience as children. These were the childhood and indeed the motherhood experiences of all those ladies so busily preparing tea for yet another Sunday School anniversary—but one which would not be full to capacity. The Sunday School only had ten children now, and they all lived some distance from the chapel. Nor could the preacher for that day really offer any hope of a more promising future.

While it is true that the thousands of chapels scattered across Britain may not have ever captured the heart of the working classes, we should not forget that many thousands of people were both influenced and helped through the worship, work and witness of such Christian communities. Even that success is easily forgotten as more and more such buildings are turned into factories, homes and even temples and mosques. Those chapels that continue to exist are often lovingly maintained. The same gloss paint is used to maintain a physical reminder of how things used to be, but it cannot recreate the culture that first built those chapels. That culture is locked in the memories of those who joined the church at that time and who today are so loyally making the Sunday School tea; but it cannot be recreated in the homes of those whose children use computers, are entertained by videos, dream of being pop stars and whose seaside visits are now prefaced by the word Costa.

In community after community, the chapel culture that seemed for so long to be a permanent feature of life in British towns and cities has changed or even moved away to be replaced by new and alien cultures. While these dramatic changes were taking place, unnoticed on a day-to-day basis, the chapels and churches which had so successfully given expression to the religious hopes and aspirations of so many were unchanging. Sometimes the refusal to change was justified on the basis that it was necessary for some things to remain the same in a world where everything else seemed to be changing. But more often the lack of change was nothing more than an inability to see how else Christian life and worship could be expressed, than in the familiar forms which had existed when the majority of those now in the church had first become members.

Those of us who come as visitors to such chapels can see all too easily the yawning chasm between what takes place in the culture of chapel life and the culture of those who live in the neighbourhood. It is as if the chapel folk are silently saying to the community: 'To become a Christian, you not only have to believe that Jesus Christ was the Son of God, that he died on a cross and was raised from the dead on the third day; you also have to find a way of living in a culture that no longer exists in everyday life.'

However, although it is very easy for us to see the cultural alienation that has taken place in situations like that we have just described, we tend not to see our own cultural blindness quite so easily. Yet our inability to see the distinction between the gospel and the cultural forms in which we express it is responsible for a great deal of the failure of the church to make a significant impact on the society of which we are a part.

So then, how can we make sense of these very different experiences of attempting to share the gospel; the one in a highly receptive Mid-West situation and the other in a chapel that had seemed to lose all contact with the world around it? Why is it the case that these experiences should be so different, when despite the cultural differences both communities are part of a modern world shaped by the achievements of a common modern, Western, Enlightenment heritage? How is it that the church in the United States can be so strong compared to the church in Europe, when it shares in a common post-Enlightenment culture? Why has secularism been able to ravage the church in Europe but not all across America? And why is it also that the experience of the mid-Western church and its close cousin, the church in the deep South, is so different from much of the rest of the church in North America, both in the parts of the United States that we have already referred to and also in Canada?

Seasoned observers of the church in the United States have several important observations to make in explanation of such paradoxes. First, it is clear that the recent history of the church in America has been vastly different from that in Europe, in that it has often been a crucial element in helping immigrant communities to define and preserve their own cultural self-understanding. The Lutheran church for Scandinavians and Germans, the Roman Catholic church for Poles, Irish, Italians and Hispanics, and the Orthodox church for Greeks, have been strongly identified not just with a set of religious beliefs but with a whole culture.

Second, as Paul Hiebert, the cultural anthropologist from Trinity College, points out, American culture—as distinct from European culture—is a great joining culture.[1] People are great voluntarists. They are persuaded of the need and value of joining organisations. The church in the United States, particularly in the Mid-West and the deep South, has been able to convince people that the church is an organisation worth joining. This may have little to do with any strongly held religious convictions. Indeed I have met those who have admitted that their primary reason for joining a particular church was to make business connections. It is virtually inconceivable that anyone would join a church in Britain for such a reason, if only because it would be a very unproductive way of making business contacts!

Third, there are those who would say that the church in the United States has not really been able to cope with secularism. What has actually happened in those parts of the country where the church is numerically strong is that it has simply welcomed a secular world view into the church, so that in terms of world view there is really no essential difference between those who have joined a particular church and those who happen to stand outside any church membership.[2] It is argued that the values espoused by crystal cathedrals, the electronic church and the prosperity gospel seem to owe more to the human potentiality movement than they do to any sense of biblical *koinonia*. In short, as Charles Taber suggests, the church has a much stronger social than religious role.[3]

Fourth, many are convinced that the likely future of the church in North America can be guessed at much more clearly by looking at the North-East and the West coast of the United States than by looking at the Mid-West and the deep South. Secular thought is making its impact felt; ethnic groups do not feel that the church is as necessary as it once was for them to preserve a feeling of cultural identity. The church is finding it harder and harder to convince people of its social value in a society which is increasingly concerned about personal fulfilment as compared with social responsibility. The United States has been, until recently, an astonishingly rural and small-town nation, but now the secularism of the cities is becoming much more influential compared with the essentially rural values of the deep South and the Mid-West. There is a noticeable difference between the attitudes of the affluent young in suburban Chicago compared with the general population in the small town, Mid-West hinterland of Chicago.

All this may well mean that the forlorn world of the chapel in Northern England is not so far distant from what might take place in many churches in the United States of America, unless a fundamental reassessment of the life and purpose of the church takes place. There is every reason for believing that despite the show of public religion, so evident at times of national crisis, the actual hearts and minds of future Americans are occupied with agendas far different from that of the gospel message. One suspects that for more and more Americans the message of the Bible seems increasingly remote and bewildering. In future days, 'the Bible says' will not be an adequate argument.[4]

The present situation of the church in North America sometimes seems rather like that of the Nonconformist church in Britain immediately prior to its dramatic decline. As William Abraham puts it, 'the pattern of decline in religion manifested in Europe is likely to spread eventually to the rest of the world.'[5]

Derek Tidball writes of the prophetic warning of one national Free Church leader at the turn of the century as that leader described the situation of the churches that he loved:

Meyer voiced the fear that the Free Churches would become a ghetto cut off from the mainstream of society, content to pay off chapel debts and to perpetuate what was called 'a comfortable pew rent Evangelical religion'. They were still too inward looking in his view and wrongly

demanded that their pastors should cater exclusively for the
needs of their own members rather than being involved in
the wider community as friend and missionary. Their services were inflexible and unattractive. Furthermore, their
evangelism had been content to perpetuate class distinctions
by creating mission halls for the working classes whilst
permitting employers to remain undisturbed at church....

Meyer had no room for the glib assumption that all the
churches needed to do was preach a simple gospel and
multitudes would willingly respond to it. He was all too
aware that secular thinking had not only penetrated the
minds of individuals but was now socially pervasive and
shaped the consciousness of the masses. The pulpit alone
would never counter that trend.[6]

The prophetic warnings of F.B. Meyer went unheeded by
British Nonconformity. However, it is still not too late for the
church in North America to learn from the unfortunate lessons
of the European experience, and indeed to learn from the
attempts of the European church of today as it attempts to
bring some measure of reform to its life and evangelistic practice.

THE RESPONSE OF THE CHURCH

In both Europe and America we can detect three major
responses of the church to the challenge of a secular world
view in the field of evangelism.

The first response has been to allow secular thought to gradually set the agenda for the church. In a powerful essay on this
subject, Paul Badham outlines the major characteristics of
such secularism within the church. He calls it a 'steady erosion
of the distinctive characteristics of Christian thought and life
among many clergy and laity who yet remain "faithful" in
terms of belonging and participation'.[7] The effect is to produce a religious faith that attempts to see its relevance in terms

of the horizons of this world but gives very little consideration to any issues relating to an eternal hope and mission.

Paul Badham points to a number of areas in the life of the church which illustrate such a process. He claims that 'the most striking instance of the secularisation of Christian thought is the widespread collapse of confidence in the rationality of belief in God amongst the clergy.'[8] The impact of such a collapse on the preaching of clergy is to produce an almost complete absence of preaching on the reasonableness of belief in God. Sermons 'concentrate instead on providing little talks about the life and work of Jesus Christ, in the context of which God can be referred to'.[9] The absence of any affirmation of the reality of God means that 'the everyday expectations of the regular Church-goer may be in practice as secularised as the expectations of the conscious atheist'.[10] In such a situation, Christian life seems to consist solely of Christians being willing 'to attend Church, listen to stories from the distant past, and modify their behaviour in accordance with the ethical teaching contained therein'.[11]

Paul Badham goes on to point out that the growth of secularisation in the church has also resulted in 'the quiet dropping of belief in a future life'.[12] The major means of reinterpreting this basic Christian doctrine is to speak about the resurrection and eternal life 'so that it is perceived as simply a way of talking about present experience within this life. There could be no greater instance of the secularisation of contemporary Christianity than its being confined to this world only. Yet this is in practice what has happened.'[13] As a consequence of such a development, the church spends a great deal of its energy focusing 'almost exclusively on the problems of this world'.[14]

While recognising that historic Christianity does have a legitimate concern for the problems of this life, Badham objects to the degree to which such concerns have come to monopolise the attention of the contemporary church. He wants to remind us that 'there is no greater dynamic for radical social change than a firm belief in transcendent and eternal values that provide a perspective from which to gain a truer evaluation of our contemporary society'.[15] Thus ironically, the concern of the church for 'relevance' actually renders it virtually indistinguishable from the secular world whose very challenge caused it to tread such a tenuous path.

A second major response of the church is not to seek to demonstrate 'relevance' so much as 'usefulness', which we might also call the utilitarian value of the church. William Abraham writes of such an outcome in this way:

> Religion, no longer the centre of life, has been driven to the margins; values are utilitarian in character or are seen as subjective in nature, and they are systematically cut loose from religious concepts and themes. In such circumstances the chances are very slim for a religion of a classical nature to flourish. At best it will remain as a leisure activity chosen by the select few on subjective grounds.[16]

In such a church, the pressure is on to make the church ever more attractive, concerned to respond to the needs that people have. In Britain, this kind of response used to be expressed as the search for the latest 'good idea', access to which would cause the church to grow. The thinking behind such a search seemed to be that since some churches did seem to be successful in terms of numerical growth, it must be possible to discover and copy the central idea which allowed them to enjoy such success. There was a failure to appreciate that what was wrong with many declining churches has little to do with their lack of a 'good idea' and everything to do with their own life and understanding of the gospel message itself.

In America, attention is focused on making the church as accessible as possible. Every amenity is offered. Convenient car parking, child-minding facilities, comfortable auditoriums, entertaining services, worship at the right time of day and of the right length. Churches seem to vie with one another in an attempt to provide the best youth facilities, the most comprehensive programmes, the finest in basketball courts. One sometimes wonders how the early church managed with only catacombs and the threat of execution if caught attending!

Obviously, one does not want to argue that churches ought to be made as uncomfortable as possible or that access to them should be made as inconvenient as one can make it, in an attempt to weed out the genuine worshipper from the frivolous attender. Indeed one can find much to admire in what is often a genuine attempt to strengthen Christian family life and to meet a whole range of human needs. But there must be something more than convenience or utility at the centre of a church's life. It is the absence of a more profound centre to the life of the church that has pushed the church to an ever more ingenious search for the latest and most imaginative attraction, sometimes presented under the slightly more acceptable title 'ministry'.

A third response can be described as the attempt to evangelise the fringes. Paul Beasley-Murray, speaking at a European Church Growth Conference in 1990, commented in passing that almost all evangelism taking place in British churches today is essentially the evangelisation of fringe members or contacts of other churches. He was not offering this as an objective account of evangelism today so much as a comment that very few churches are able to conduct evangelism designed to reach those who stand outside any religious tradition.

The attempt to evangelise the fringes of church life, whether our own fringe or the fringes of other churches, comes in a variety of forms. One manifestation is to concentrate more and more on evangelistic techniques or programmes. There is a considerable variety of methods available to churches ranging from local visitation programmes to larger-scale events. Even the crusade approach to evangelism is largely an appeal to fringe contacts that the church has already made. Research undertaken during crusades held in Great Britain in the 1980s found that less than 10% of converts came to a crusade meeting on their own as a consequence of the high profile of the crusade. The overwhelming majority of converts came because they were invited by someone from a local church.

Church Growth teaching has a means of categorising the –

natural contacts of each church member. The usual classifica-
tion is to speak in terms of contacts made through work,
school, family, neighbours, friends known socially and uncon-
verted church attenders. Each of these contacts is seen as a
potential way of expanding the fringe contacts of the church.
Possibly the most effective use of programmes such as Evangelism Explosion is to apply them to training Christians in the
evangelisation of fringe members.

A slightly different variation of the growth of the 'fringes
approach' is one often practised by churches with a broadly
charismatic life and character. We might call this the 'growth
by attractive worship' theory. I have to confess that having
been nurtured in the delightful worship of the Fisherfolk in
the 1970s and more recently in the contemporary style of
writers such as Graham Kendrick, I have more than a little
bias towards such a view. However, while there have undoubt-
edly been many fine churches which have grown through such
an ethos, it is still hard to argue that such growth extends very
far beyond reaching those who might fall broadly within a
church-based culture, even if they had never made a personal
commitment to Christ before their involvement in a charismatic church.

It is perhaps unfortunate that in Britain the most persuasive
model for such an approach within the historic churches has
been that of St Michael-le-Belfrey in York. I do not use the
word 'unfortunate' as a criticism of St Michael's—far from it.
My knowledge of that congregation and its witness leaves me
full of admiration. However, I fear that many who do not
know the congregation well are left with the impression that
their growth has come primarily through the quality of their
worship life. Such an impression does not adequately take
account of the very powerful evangelistic gifts of the vicar,
David Watson, under whose ministry the church grew so
dramatically.

In more recent years those who have espoused such a view
have looked to the 'signs and wonders' movement associated
with John Wimber, as a continuation of the 'evangelisation
through worship' theme. Again, one cannot deny the power of

many of the meetings that take place under the ministry of John Wimber and others associated with him. Indeed, not only have I been present myself at such meetings but I have heard first-hand accounts of those who have been converted at such meetings. However, I still want to raise the question as to whether or not such an emphasis actually moves very far beyond those who are broadly familiar with a church-based culture.

This is not to trivialise the potential of reaching out to those who have had significant contact with a church at some point in their lives. There are still many such people in our society. An assessment made on the basis of responses to Gallup polls suggests that in Britain, the church could potentially double its size by reaching out successfully to this group of people. Since not all congregations would be likely to grow equally by such means, it follows that some individual congregations could grow significantly by reaching out to such people. However we need to remember that in a society which is increasingly being impacted by the forces of secularism, this group is becoming smaller as time passes. More seriously, young people are less and less likely to be part of this group in our culture. Interestingly it is young people who are largely absent from any church in Europe, whether charismatic or not.

In my travels throughout the British Isles I come across many growing churches. It is a privilege to be able to talk with the leaders of such churches and to consider with them the factors that have caused their churches to grow. Most if not all of these leaders are deeply committed to the extension of the kingdom of God. Whenever I am able to hold such conversations I want to know how many of those who have joined their church have come as transfers, either from other churches or because they are Christians who have recently moved into the area; and how many have become Christians having made a first-time commitment to Christ in the context of their church. I am also interested to know how many who have made first-time commitments have done so from a totally unchurched background. I remember with deep affection those individuals to whom I have been introduced who have come from a totally unchurched background. Many have told me their stories, a few have seen a good number of their family come to Christ. Some of those that I know are members of my own church.

However, I am also aware that these individuals are almost always exceptions and that the overwhelming majority of people who are added to the churches that I have visited have come as transfers, or as people who have found their way back to faith after some or many years of inactive Christian lives. I realise that my travels do not represent an objective survey of the means by which people have been added to churches. Yet when I add to my own experiences those of the many other Christian leaders that I question concerning their knowledge of churches that are growing, I find it difficult to believe that my experiences are not very representative of church life in Britain.

My travels in other European countries and in the United States are not nearly as comprehensive as they have been in Great Britain, and yet they echo very closely what I have seen in my own land. It is clear from looking at the evangelistic programmes of churches that the intention of most programmes is to attempt to invite people to one or other of the activities (usually a worship service) held by a local church. These attempts to invite others to our existing programmes certainly have some effect in lively churches; but I question how valuable such a strategy will be in terms of reaching those beyond the fringe of any church.

My family includes a fairly inactive Labrador. For reasons I can never fully understand, it seems to have become almost exclusively my job to walk the dog. As I have walked the dog over the last two years, I have discovered that dog owners talk easily to each other. Somehow the common experience of owning a dog allows people to overcome their apparently natural English reserve. A whole variety of conversations has brought home to me very powerfully the reality that large numbers of people in my community have no significant relationship with any church. Moreover, no matter how attractive our worship services, no matter how welcoming our congregation, it is extremely unlikely that many, if any, of the good folk that I meet on my dog walks are ever likely to turn up at any worship service—with or without their dog!

Yet this does not mean that these same people are not asking essentially religious questions; our conversations have shown me that they are. We have to face the fact that when people are searching for a God encounter, the church is not an institution that comes readily to mind. Indeed, some give the impression that the church is almost the last place where they would expect to find God. My own experience, combined with the experience of others, suggests to me that the overwhelming majority of people in our communities can only be reached if the church takes an initiative to meet them where they are. If we continue to operate strategies which depend on waiting for people to come to us we will be disappointed. They simply will not come.

It is true that there are some churches that have a significant involvement in the life of the community in which they are set. Some key leaders have been able to build sensitive and creative contacts with their community which we might describe as the building of bridges between church and community. However I really do wonder how many people we can really expect to cross such bridges, and how much weight we can really expect such bridges to bear.

A CHURCH FOR OTHERS

The problem of the church from its earliest days until now has been the tension that exists between the concern of the church for itself, its own life and members and its proper focus on the mission given to it by God. As David Bosch puts it in his epic work on mission:

> Mission is missio Dei, which seeks to subsume into itself the missiones ecclasiae, the missionary programs of the church. It is not the church which 'undertakes' mission; it is the missio Dei which constitutes the church. The mission of the church needs constantly to be renewed and re-conceived.[18]

What is really needed is not more effective bridges to bring people back to our churches, so much as a new kind of church that does not have the kind of cultural barriers in the first place—barriers that then require the careful construction of bridges to allow people access to our cultural enclaves. The only kind of bridges that we really need are those that allow the church to move into the community, to be recreated in the midst of those alienated communities that we are seeking to reach so that the church becomes genuinely the church of God for them.

There is some evidence that such churches are beginning to emerge, and in the third part of this book we will look at a few projects which have some of the signs of being such churches. They are by no means the only examples of what God is doing in and through his church, but they are pointers to that more general activity. However, the temptation for all of us in looking at specific models or indeed in considering these issues in general is that our attention should be drawn too much to the specifics of particular programmes. To be sure, we are concerned for the 'nuts and bolts' of particular programmes but we must be careful not to be tempted to think that we can look at programmes and then copy them. We are concerned here to look at the life of the church. Life cannot be imitated, it must be lived!

The life that we are called to is nothing less than the life of Jesus renewing his church, calling his church to ever fresh challenges, challenging his church to reflect more of his life in its life, and offering to his church a participation in that mission which is his mission. Speaking of the role of the local church as God's partner in mission, Lesslie Newbigin looks for local churches that are willing to 'renounce an introverted concern for their own life, and recognize that they exist for the sake of those who are not members, as signs, instrument, and foretaste of God's redeeming grace for the whole life of society'.[19]

It is this kind of church, the church of Jesus coming into being as a church for others, that we want to describe and reflect on.

FOOTNOTES

1. Paul Hiebert made this observation in response to a question that I put to him during a private conversation held at Bible House, Swindon, in April 1991.

2. This point is made very well by the American missiologist, Charles Taber in an unpublished manuscript, *Issues in Mission* (23 March 1991), p 10, in the possession of this author.

3. Paul Hiebert's view of the American people as great voluntarists is reinforced in the paper cited above.

4. The phrase 'the Bible says' is one that is strongly associated with the preaching of Billy Graham.

5. William Abraham, *The Logic of Evangelism* (Hodder and Stoughton: 1989), p 188.

6. Derek Tidball, ' "A Work so Rich in Promise"; the 1901 Simultaneous Mission and the Failure of Co-operative Evangelism', available as an extract from the author, p 99.

7. Paul Badham, 'Some Secular Trends in the Church of England Today', Paul Badham (ed), *Religion, State, and Society in Modern Britain* (Edwin Mellen Press: 1989), p 23.

8. *Ibid*, p 24.

9. *Ibid*, p 25.

10. *Ibid*, p 26.

11. *Ibid*.

12. *Ibid*.

13. *Ibid*, p 26f.

14. *Ibid*, p 28.

15. *Ibid*, p 31.

16. William Abraham, *op cit*, p 188.

17. For a discussion on the mission entrusted by God to the early church see M. Robinson and S. Christine, *Planting Tomorrow's Churches Today* (Monarch: 1992), Chapter 1.

18. David Bosch, *Transforming Mission* (Orbis: 1991), p 519.

19. Lesslie Newbigin, *The Gospel in a Pluralist Society* (SPCK: 1989), p 233.

CHAPTER THREE

A *Church For the Unchurched*

A SMALL GROUP OF CHURCH LEADERS had gathered in a
room in central London. Each had come in response to
the same kind of personal invitation that I had
received.[1] As I entered the room I realised that I knew most of
those present by name or reputation. The one man that I did
not know was the quiet American that we had all come to
meet. Jerry Butler was the Director of International Ministries
at a church set in the suburbs of Chicago, Willow Creek
Community Church. All of us present in the room that day
had read something of this church; what we had read interested us enough to want to learn more.

Jerry began to speak. He told of his interest in evangelism
and of how in the past, when he had detected some interest in
the Christian message on the part of his unchurched friends,
he had often hesitated to take them to church. More than that,
he had often wanted to make sure that they were soundly
converted before he had dared to risk exposing them to the
church. My interest was warming! I thought back to my first
church and to the evangelistic strategy that we had used. In
that situation, we had seen a number of people converted
through small home study groups, before they ever came near
our church. Even twenty years ago, I had known instinctively

that such an approach was necessary for those who were completely unchurched.

I was ready to hear more but was unprepared for the
devastating simplicity of the message. 'Imagine a church service which is designed for those who don't go to church,' said
Jerry. Yes! I was starting to imagine it and I knew that it
would look quite unlike anything that we did in my own
church.

Just over six months after this initial meeting with Jerry
Butler I found myself attending a ministers' conference at
Willow Creek Community Church. There were around 1,300
other clergy and church leaders present. Most were from the
United States but there were a number from other countries,
including a good sprinkling from European countries. A ripple
of laughter wafted across the auditorium as the 1,300 leaders
identified with the speaker's message. Bill Hybels, the Senior
Pastor at Willow Creek, was telling his story with considerable
panache. He was reflecting on his teenage years. He recalled
how on one occasion one of his best friends, someone who was
well respected by his peers, had expressed some interest in the
Christian message. In a moment of bad judgement he had
invited his friend to a church service. He recounted in detail
his embarrassment at what had followed. The poor music
programme, so poor that his friend was wondering why no-one
was throwing things at the musician; the obscure language;
the sermon that was so incomprehensible that you wondered if
the preacher had any idea at all of what he was trying to say.

Following this experience, Bill's friend avoided him for a
few days. When he eventually tracked him down, Bill asked
him what was wrong. His response made a significant impression on the young Bill Hybels: 'I had always thought of you as
normal, but what you took me to was not normal.' Needless to
say, any interest in the Christian message ceased at that point.
That kind of experience, together with many others, was
clearly formative for anyone who had a strong interest in
leading others, particularly those of his own generation, to
Christ.

THE IMPACT OF WILLOW CREEK

'Are you from the church?' asked the waitress on hearing our English accents. There was no question about which church she had in mind. Certainly there were other churches in the area, but she had in mind one particular church.

Another night, another restaurant. 'You're very busy tonight,' we observed. 'Yes, we're always busy on a Wednesday night. The church has a meeting on a Wednesday.' She seemed to assume that we knew which church she meant. I wondered to myself: What kind of church could so dramatically affect the restaurant trade, and make so much impact on the immediate area that it was not even mentioned by name—it was just *the church*?

We had just come from the church in question, having attended their midweek celebration along with some thousands of others. Willow Creek Community Church was certainly a talking point in the area. The sheer impact of the numbers ensured that everyone in the area was aware of its presence.

The present day statistics of Willow Creek Community Church are impressive, especially to a European. The second-largest church in North America, it is reputedly the fastest growing Protestant church in that continent. Around 15,000 people attend the week-end services, while around 6,000 attend the mid-week New Community worship services. The full- and part-time staff, who number almost 300, could comprise a good-sized church on their own. The campus in which the church is set comprises 130 acres of land. The facilities in the building are maintained at the highest possible standard without being opulent, and are continually improving.

But one can soon absorb statistics and after a time become used to the great size of Willow Creek. I suspect that what really attracts people at this unusual church is not something that can be captured very easily on paper. I can perhaps start to describe this 'X factor' by calling it a kind of raw energy. It is this raw, creative drive that has allowed the unusual to happen.

Bill Hybels has said that they did not set out to be, or to create, a large church. Rather, Hybels believes that they had a threefold focus. First was an intention to create a church that reflected what it meant to be a biblical community, in which there would be transparent loving relationships. He comments that America does not need more big churches, but it does need more biblical churches. Second came a commitment to have as a primary focus of the church the attempt to reach those who stand outside of any existing Christian commitment. There is no interest in sheep-swapping, although Hybel concedes 'a few have leaked in. What can you do?' he asks apologetically. Third was a conviction that the cause of Christ is sufficiently important to demand a high quality of commitment and effort on the part of those who follow him.[2]

Willow Creek authentically reflects those kinds of concerns. One senses that the kind of tough idealism that emerges in such priorities began before the church itself was started. To understand what drives Willow Creek, it is essential to capture some of the flavour of its youthful predecessor.

THE CREATIVITY OF YOUTH

The story of Willow Creek begins in an unusually creative partnership forged in the youth ministry of South Park Church in Park Ridge, Illinois, a Chicago suburb.[3] This was an interdenominational church of some 400 members. The music director was a man named Glenn Jorian. The church wanted to start a second Sunday-morning service with a contemporary feel. Glenn Jorian invited his occasional accompanist, an unusually talented pianist named Dave Holmbo, to help him with the musical ingredient in this slightly different service.

After some time working in the church Dave Holmbo had the idea of assembling a singing group composed of young people in the church, which he was to call the 'Son Company'. Before long he decided to put on a concert as a showcase for his new group and enlisted the help of a number of friends whom he had met some time before and had recently turned up at one of the church services. Bill Hybels was one of them; after a short time, he joined the staff of South Park Church as the

Youth Pastor. At that time, the youth group numbered some 25 kids, but with the help of the highly creative energies of Bill Hybels and Dave Holmbo, something very unusual was to emerge.

The creative genesis for what was beginning to emerge took place around a Bible study run by Bill Hybels for the young people, immediately following the Son Company rehearsals. Over a short period of time, the number of young people attending these events grew from around 30 to 80. This growth gave birth to the idea that it might be possible to separate the music rehearsal time from the Bible study time and then to hold a special evening when existing members of the group could invite their friends to a gospel presentation. The presentation would include the kind of contemporary music that they were already developing. They also dreamed of adding other ingredients such as multi-media, music and drama presentations.

The resulting attendance greatly exceeded their expectations. Somewhere between 150 and 200 young people came on that first night. More critically for Bill Hybels, who presented the message, a large number of those who came made a clear commitment to Christ. As Bill Hybels tells it, the experience helped him to define very clearly what he wanted to do from then on. As you might expect, the leaders were not inclined to stop with just one event. The mid-week 'Son City', as it became known, grew within six months to an attendance of 300. Having begun the first event in 1973, by the summer of 1974 the group had grown to some 500 and was soon making the decision to meet on two separate nights to accommodate the numbers that wanted to come. By 1975 somewhere between 1,000 and 1,500 young people were attending and the budget had grown from an original youth budget of $300 to one of $80,000. The programme had also become more sophisticated, with a distinction being made between those who were still coming as 'seekers' and those who needed discipleship.

No youth ministry continues completely unchanged, and by 1975 the creative, essential principles of a culturally relevant and effective presentation of the gospel, coupled with an effective discipleship programme that then went on to recognise and use the gifts of those who were being discipled, had been established.

Not only had critical principles been established, but a key group of team members had also been welded together in the heat of the challenges that had been tackled. Their success in seeing the highly improbable come into being had transformed a talented group of individuals into possibility thinkers. No task was too great, no dream unthinkable. A good number of the key team members from that period are still leaders at Willow Creek today. Not the least of these are Nancy Beach, the production director (who was a member of the original group of 25 young people from South Park Church); Don Cousins, now the Associate Pastor and primary leader of the staff, who was recruited in the Son City days; and Dr Gilbert Bilezikian, the church's founding elder, who was the inspirational mentor who had strongly influenced Bill Hybels while still a student at Trinity College, Illinois.

The question that then arose was simply 'Where to from here?' To some extent, the question had been forced by the pressure that such a high activity and high-profile ministry had placed on the life of the South Park church. Toleration had its limits and they were being reached. The answer came in the recognition that many of the young people who had become Christians had parents who had not been reached with the gospel. Might it be possible to find a culturally relevant presentation of the gospel that could reach adults? That was certainly the direction that many in the group felt that God was leading them to explore.

UNCHURCHED HARRY, UNCHURCHED MARY

Approximately 100 of the Son City young people shared with Bill Hybels and Dave Holmbo their vision to reach adults with the Christian message. Their first task was a little unorthodox; I do not think you will find it in the pages of most church planting manuals. The team of 100 began to sell tomatoes door-to-door! The reason was simple. They needed money for basic items such as sound equipment, and since Bill Hybels came from a family that sold farm products such an approach offered a solution. Dave Holmbo and Bill Hybels had both left their staff positions at South Park and were trying to support themselves by means of a variety of part time jobs. Money was in short supply!

The second task was much more orthodox; you can find it in many manuals on church planting, although it is surprising how few actually do it. They decided to undertake a survey of a representative sample of those who were living in the part of North-Western suburban Chicago that they had selected for their church planting venture. The survey was designed to find those who did not attend any church, to see if they could find out why they did not and, just as importantly, to see if they could discover what would make them more likely to do so. The survey made some surprising discoveries. The most often cited reason given by people for not attending church was that the church was always asking for money. Other reasons were listed as follows:

I am unable to relate to the music.
The message is irrelevant to my life.
The church does not meet my needs.
The services are predictable and boring.
The church makes me feel guilty.[4]

Just as important, the survey also asked the question, 'If these factors were eliminated, would you then consider going to church?' A good number answered 'Yes' to that question. Those who did were informed that such a church was going to start soon and they were given the relevant details.

The survey not only helped them to think through the kind of event that the team would make the centrepiece of their outreach, it also helped them to obtain a feel for the kind of people that they wanted to reach with the gospel. Another way of expressing that awareness is that the emerging group had made a conscious decision to target a particular group of people in the community.

The kind of person that Willow Creek was targetting could be defined as a professional male, aged 25 to 45 who is married, actively involved in the commercial world and disenchanted with the traditional church. That profile, together with their families, described a very large number of people in the community which they had selected for their church plant. The decision to specifically target men, rather than the more diverse target of family, arose from the observation that most churches had difficulty in reaching men. The strategy of many churches was to accept the fact that it was easier to reach women than men and then to hope that having reached women, it would be possible to help them to reach their husbands. In some cases, churches would even target children in the hope that parents could be reached through contact with their offspring. The reality often is that such strategies actually help to reinforce the view of men, that church is for women and children and has little relevance for those who have now grown up and have to survive in the business community. A decision to target men operates on the basis that it is much more likely that whole families will become involved through the commitment of the husband than through the commitment of the wife.

The group went on to formulate a clearer picture of what such people believed. They noticed that it was unlikely that such a person would have any existing contact with any church and even less likely that they would be thinking about attending any church. If they were aware of having any spiritual needs, it is probable that they would be looking at ways other than the Christian faith to meet those needs; but they would be more likely to be unaware of having explicitly religious needs. Their world view would be largely secular; and although there might be some residual Christian value system, it would not necessarily be recognised as being anything more than the cultural norm.

Clearly, such thinking is controversial. The very notion of any kind of targetting leaves many committed Christians feeling very uncomfortable. The conviction of many Christians is that the church should be available for anyone in a given community. Christ died 'once and for all', therefore we do not have any right to limit the revelation of his love to a particular group. Moreover, many Christians would want to point to the church in the New Testament, particularly to cosmopolitan churches such as that at Corinth, as examples of highly diverse groups of believers. Many Christians might want to say that a commitment to a multi-ethnic church which contains people of very different socio-economic groups is essential if the church is ever going to model to the world what it means to be 'a colony of heaven here on earth'. The church is the new community of God that allows such human barriers to be crossed.

However, such a view tends to overlook the fact that not every church in the New Testament was like that in practice. There is increasingly strong evidence to suggest that the division between, for example, Jewish and Gentile Christians was in fact very strong.[5] Moreover, evidence from both the historic and contemporary church suggests that very few local congregations are able to accommodate a wide range of social groups within a single congregation.

This does not mean that those who are Christians should refrain from attempting to bring down such barriers. Even more, it is clearly not reflective of New Testament Christianity to deliberately erect barriers designed to keep people out. Churches which actively prevent people attending on the basis of cultural or racial criteria are clearly operating outside the norms of historic Christianity.

However, to say that one wishes to reach a particular group of people, especially if those people are unreached because no church currently exists which operates within their cultural setting, is not the same thing as seeking to exclude others. To argue that targetting significant groups of people who are alienated from the church is to erect cultural barriers would be like arguing that the original Jewish church should not have made the necessary cultural changes which were needed in order to reach Gentile unbelievers−for fear of excluding any Jewish people who might have wanted to become believers.

Clearly, while in principle anyone who might want to join a particular congregation must be free to do so, and while the global church must find ways of being as inclusive of every cultural, racial and socio-economic group as possible, every local expression of the church is going to be socially and culturally conditioned to some extent. The only question is the degree to which a church is able to recognise the group that it is reaching as compared with the group that it believes God is calling it to reach.

For Willow Creek, not only does the group that they are seeking to reach form a very large part of the largely homogeneous middle-class community in which they are set, but those they seek to reach are people who are very similar to those who formed the core group of the church. As Bill Hybels puts it: 'Generally a pastor can define his appropriate target audience by determining with whom he would like to spend a vacation or an afternoon of recreation.'[6] There are clearly many in the immediate community with whom the various members of the original core group at Willow Creek would feel very comfortable. The only essential difference between those who worship at Willow Creek and those who live in the community is simply the factor of Christian commitment. There are no other cultural barriers to overcome. Those who fit such a description and are therefore part of the target audience are called by Willow Creek 'unchurched Harry and unchurched Mary'. The church has become well known for keeping a clear focus in terms of what such people are like.

There is almost no better example of unchurched Harry than the man who is currently Willow Creek's Director of Communication and one of their teaching pastors: Lee Strobel. In 1980, Strobel was the legal affairs editor of the Chicago Tribune. He was absorbed in a career that was deeply fulfilling, was well paid and saw no need for God in his world. To quote Strobel, 'I was an atheist. I just thought that the idea of God was ridiculous. I'm a very skeptical person. My background is in journalism and law, so you've got to prove it to me, and the idea of God just sounded absurd.'[7]

Interestingly, in Strobel's case he first attended the church because his wife, who had very closely fitted the profile of unchurched Mary, had started attending a year earlier and had encouraged him to 'check it out'. When he first attended, he said, 'I didn't want anyone to see me in church. I used to carry a notebook with me so in case someone I knew spotted me, I could say I was working on a story.'[8] There are probably very few churches that someone like Lee Strobel would have felt able to attend, and even fewer that he would have returned to sufficiently often to really consider the message that was being presented.

However, the targetting that Willow Creek engages in has a strategic ingredient beyond that of simply reaching those people who they feel to be most like themselves. Their conviction is that the effective reaching of this people-group will be critical in terms of seeking to communicate the gospel to the whole of society. For Willow Creek, targetting one particular group does not comprise their whole mission; rather, it is only a starting point from which to reach many groups, all of whom matter equally to God.

THE CHURCH IS LAUNCHED

The first Seeker's Service was launched on 12 October 1975 in a rented movie theatre called the Willow Creek Theater in a suburb of Chicago known as Palatine. The name of the theatre shaped the name of the church–Willow Creek Community Church. The film that was showing later that day was still emblazoned above the entrance: *Everything You Ever Wanted to Know About Sex, But Were Afraid to Ask*. The initial attendance was around 125 people. The congregation was composed largely of the original group of approximately 100 young people from the Son City contingent, and most of the rest were the parents whom they had dragged along to church. This was no longer a mid-week evening event but a Sunday morning occasion, intended for adults.

Anyone who has ever worshipped in a church that uses rented facilities will understand that even under normal circumstances a rented facility presents tremendous problems for those who are responsible for the logistics of a service. The scale of the inventive approach to outreach attempted by the new church stretched the core group to the limit. The fifteenth anniversary edition of the Willow Creek magazine describes the extent of the commitment necessary to make the event happen:

> There was that sense of abandonment to the cause and ownership of ministry. On Sunday morning–early Sunday morning–that was especially apparent. Joel Jager, for example, was in charge of a team of volunteers who would set up lights and sound equipment at the theater. After working 60 hours or so in a tool and die shop during the week, Jager would get up at 4 a.m., load up one of Harold Hybels' old produce trucks and, if it would start, arrive at the theater at 5.30 a.m. About eight to 10 volunteers would arrive to unload and set up.
>
> As the church grew, an 11 a.m. service was added. Often, the theater would show an early matinee at 12:15 p.m. Jager's crew would literally have to run the equipment outside, even in the dead of winter, just to get out in time. They would then break down the equipment in the freezing cold or a scorching sun and then load it on the truck.[9]

After one year more than 1,000 people were attending the weekend services. By 1979 that number had almost doubled and the facilities were hardly able to keep pace with the growth that had taken place. Two years before, in 1977, a start had been made in raising money to build their own facility which, after at least one frustrated attempt to buy land, was located in a suburb a few miles away from the movie theatre.

The period between the decision to fund-raise and the actual date of the new facility opening in 1981 represented a coming of age for the infant church. Many painful problems were encountered including the breakdown of some key relationships, due in part to the intense pressure under which many of the leaders were operating. In particular, the creative relationship between Dave Holmbo and Bill Hybels ended. Dave Holmbo left the church following problems in his personal life. In referring to this time, Bill Hybels has commented, 'We were always just one New Community away from extinction.'[10] The youthful pioneers were learning the difference between running a successful youth ministry under the auspices of another church and creating their own ministry among adults. It was not an easy transition.

In a presentation at a church leadership conference held by Willow Creek, Don Cousins includes a time when he speaks under the general heading of 'Mistakes that we made'. For those with ears to hear, this very frank admission of human frailty—much of which dates from this period—is both refreshing and creative. The pain of some rather fundamental mistakes helped to lay some significant foundations for the future of the church. The Willow Creek magazine writing of this time comments:

> There were crucial changes: the elders, tried under fire, became the ruling body of the church. The staff took on a well-defined reporting structure to make accountability possible. Expectations for staff and leaders were outlined: no longer would it be enough to just have a spiritual gift or proficiency. The pace was allowed to slow down. Relationships and caring for people, once again, were the core of the church.[11]

The opening of the new facility, early on in a new decade, allowed the church to have a sense of a new beginning. The continued growth of Willow Creek through that decade brought to the church a profile, not just in the immediate community but in the national church life of North America. Writing about Willow Creek in a book entitled *10 of Today's Most Innovative Churches*, Elmer Towns says of the church that it is:

> One of the most innovative churches in America because of its creative programming and, more importantly, because of its unique philosophy of ministry and its well-thought-out strategy for reaching the unchurched.[12]

A STRATEGY DEFINED

The stability that the church enjoyed as it entered both its new facility and the new decade of the 1980s allowed it to reflect on the strategy that it had adopted from the early Son City days and formulate it in a thought-through seven-step philosophy designed to reach unchurched Harry and Mary.[13] The seven steps are as follows:

1. Building authentic relationships

Many experts in evangelism and church growth recognise that the time when most Christians have the greatest number of friendships with the unchurched is when they first become Christians. For very understandable reasons, there is a tendency for most Christians to gradually lose those relationships, finding greater fulfilment in friendships with other Christians. As this process continues there often comes a time when many Christians find that they have no significant relationships with any who are not also Christians. Willow Creek therefore encourages their members to deliberately cultivate friendships with those who are not Christians.

By their very nature, authentic relationships with the unchurched cannot be ones which are shallow, manipulative friendships with the sole intention of bringing that person to Christ. However much a person might want to see someone make such a decision, the basis of the friendship cannot lie in such a desire. There must also be a genuine concern for the well-being of others, however they respond to the Christian message. Such an emphasis not only has an implication for the task of evangelism, but carries with it an expectation of the degree to which Christians will be active participants in the society of which they are part. Regardless of any direct evangelistic implication, the participation of Christians in the kind of activity needed to form such relationships helps to produce a well-rounded lifestyle, allowing Christians genuinely to act as salt in the world.

2. Sharing a verbal witness

There is a confusion in the minds of many Christians between evangelism and witness. The New Testament makes it clear that evangelism is a specific gift and not all Christians should expect to have such a gift. The well-known researcher in Church Growth, Peter Wagner, has estimated that in the normal Christian community we might expect to find that some 10% of people have the gift of evangelism.[14]

However, Wagner and others point to the fact that while only some might expect to have the gifting necessary to make them an effective evangelist, all should expect to be able to function as witnesses 'ready at all times to answer anyone who asks you to explain the hope that you have in you, but do it with gentleness and respect' (1 Peter 3:15,16). Eddie Gibbs further describes a witness as 'someone who can and is ready to speak from personal experience of what Christ has done in his life. This verbal witness stems from the silent witness of a quality of life which demands an explanation.'[15]

3. Providing a Service for Seekers

This feature of Willow Creek is the one that has probably attracted more attention than any other. The fundamental concept is one of a covenant or partnership between the church and its members. All too often churches encourage their members to speak to others about Christ, without really offering a helpful context in which that initial witness can be further developed.

The conviction of Willow Creek is that it is possible to produce a forum that is sufficiently attractive for Christians to want to invite their friends to attend, as opposed to one that they would rather protect their friends from. Such an approach has its critics even within the evangelical community. The leadership of Willow Creek has expressed its deep sense of hurt at the comments of those who have inaccurately accused them of offering entertainment in place of proclamation.

4. Attendance at the New Community Service

Willow Creek recognises that the needs of believers are different from those of unbelievers. It is therefore essential that the church should offer an opportunity for worship which is specifically intended to meet the needs of committed believers in worship. The New Community Service, held on two evenings in the mid-week, represents the next step for those who have begun to attend the weekend Seeker Service and have made a commitment to be a follower of Jesus. The main focus of this event is therefore worship, teaching and a once-a-month celebration of communion.

5. Participation in a Small Group

The importance of small groups in the life of a growing church has been strongly affirmed by many researchers in Church Growth. The value of such groups lies both in the area of discipleship and pastoral care. In the context of Willow Creek, discipleship-making small groups usually consist of 8-10 people who meet weekly for a period of two years. The study programme for small groups comes from a curriculum produced by Willow Creek and is strongly relational in nature. Other small groups are formed around the accomplishment of specific tasks or exist to assimilate people into the church.

6. Involvement in ministry

The writer Elton Trueblood is credited with the rather startling statement that he is in favour of the abolition of the laity. By this, Trueblood meant that the Christian gospel is intended to produce a community of believers each of which has a clear call to the ministry of service. Willow Creek encourages Christians who attend church to discover, develop and deploy their God-given gift of ministry, believing that only through such a course of action will each believer be able to fulfil his or her spiritual potential.

7. The exercise of stewardship

It is not uncommon for Protestant churches of an evangelical persuasion to teach and promote the principle of the tithing of income. In the context of Willow Creek such a principle extends to helping each member in the management of resources as part of a total lifestyle. This not only allows significant resources to be available for the extension of ministry, it is also seen as part of the production of a distinctive Christian witness through lifestyle.

Encouraging believers to be committed to a Christian lifestyle enables the issue of an authentic witness to be part of the building of authentic relationships. So the seven-step philosophy of Willow Creek is intended to come full cycle, continually raising the issue of outreach to the unchurched. In such an atmosphere of commitment it is not surprising that Willow Creek has gained its reputation as a church which has experienced significant growth.

By this criterion, many would be tempted to call Willow Creek a successful church. However, it is interesting to see the extent to which Bill Hybels deliberately resists such a description. He has strongly expressed the view that it is foolish to talk of success in a situation where despite the numbers of people attending Willow Creek, large numbers of people stand well outside the influence of any church, let alone that of Willow Creek. Hybels believes that there are at least 300,000 unchurched people within their catchment area, apart from the many millions across North America who are well outside the reach of Willow Creek.

Where might Willow Creek go from here? Certainly there are physical constraints on the growth of Willow Creek. In the Autumn of 1991 a fourth identical weekend service was added, to form a pattern of two services on a Saturday evening and two on a Sunday. Although the addition of this extra service adds some extra capacity for the church to grow, the current figure of some 15,000 people attending on a weekend comes close to the realistic limits for the size of the facility that they presently have.

Nor is it just a matter of adding to the existing building; the sheer movement of that number of people to and from the building has produced significant strains on the road system in the immediate area. Recently, the inclusion of a high-profile speaker on the programme produced such a high attendance that it took one-and-a-half hours for some of those who attended to get clear of the parking area!

Church planting in neighbouring areas might be one option for future development. Recently, there has come a proposal to establish an Association that would encourage the development of more 'seeker sensitive' churches across the United States. The International ministry that Jerry Butler has pioneered is unearthing a high degree of interest in similar approaches in other lands. Whatever new developments come, the one common theme is not just the general theme of growth, but the specific theme of developing those strategies which lead to the completely unchurched being reached for the extension of the Kingdom of God.

FOOTNOTES

1. The meeting in question was held at Westminster Central Hall London in the Autumn of 1990. It had been called by David Coffey who is now General Secretary of the Baptist Union.

2. These points are taken directly from a taped message by Bill Hybels, 'Building a Church for the Unchurched', given at the Church Leaders' Conference held at Willow Creek in May 1991.

3. The information on the origins of Willow Creek is taken from 'Laying the Foundations', *Willow Creek Magazine* vol 2 no 2 (Nov/Dec 1990): pp 12ff.

4. The responses to the survey are printed in a paper produced by Willow Creek Community Church and entitled *Overview*.

5. There is an increasing number of books being published at the moment emphasising the Jewish origins of Christianity. In doing so, they highlight the tension that existed between the Jewish roots and the later Gentile mission of the church. A useful summary of one aspect of this debate, namely the interaction of the church with the 'Godfearers', can be found in J. Andrew Overman, 'The God-Fearers: Some Neglected Features', *Journal for the Study of the New Testament* 32 (1988): pp 17-26.

6. Elmer Towns, *10 of Today's Most Innovative Churches* (Regal: 1990), p 48.

7. Tom Valeo, 'Hybels: Why do 12,000 people listen to this man each week?', *Daily Herald, Suburban Living section* (18 May 1988): p 2.

8. *Ibid*.

9. 'The Theater Days', *Willow Creek Magazine* vol 2 no 2 (Nov/Dec 1990): p 31.

10. *Ibid*, p 38.

11. *Ibid*.

12. Elmer Towns, *op cit*, p 44.

13. Information on the seven-step strategy is taken from the paper cited in note 4.

14. Eddie Gibbs, *I Believe in Church Growth* (Hodder and Stoughton: rev edn 1990), p 200.

15. *Ibid*, p 198.

CHAPTER FOUR

A *Safe Place*
For a Dangerous Message

THE PRESENTATION MADE BY Jerry Butler of Willow Creek to a small group of church leaders in London during the Autumn of 1990 was the first time that most of those present had understood in any detail the strategy of that church. A number of those who had been present began to share with others what they had heard. The idea of a church designed for those who did not come rather than for those who were already members produced a variety of responses. Some were incredulous, some excited, others stimulated, but few thought it unthinkable. In almost every case the idea struck people as original and yet, when they had heard it, as obvious. It was particularly telling to observe the reaction of those who were the leaders of churches that were already growing and who had a reputation for evangelistic outreach.

Nearly all of these leaders quickly offered the view that although their churches were involved in evangelism and were seeing people make commitments of faith, few of the converts were from a totally unchurched background. Most acknowledged that they really had been very unsuccessful in seeing the completely unchurched touched by the Christian message.

HAVE WE ALWAYS IGNORED THE UNCHURCHED?

Even though it has been encouraging to see such responses, it is important to recognise that the fundamental concept embodied by the Seeker Service strategy, that of creating an environment for the completely unchurched, is not actually as completely new as it sounds. In both Britain and America it has been common practice for more than 150 years for churches within an evangelical tradition to have both a morning and evening church service, each of which originally had a very different purpose. The morning was traditionally for believers and the evening service for the preaching of the gospel.

Even before evangelical churches developed such a pattern of worship, the older churches in Europe had a pattern of morning and evening worship. To some extent, this was an inheritance from an older medieval pattern of worship, which in turn was largely shaped by the monastic tradition of Christendom. In such a setting all worship services were designed entirely to meet the needs of Christians because in the context of Christendom, everyone was regarded as at least nominally Christian. Worship was therefore a duty for all, a duty often encouraged by state legislation. The concept of worship as a place for encouraging a Christian commitment on the part of those who were not Christians was unknown.

Later, under the influence of the revival movements in both Britain and America, and as it became apparent that many in society were not committed Christians, the content of preaching changed dramatically. Initially such evangelistic preaching was conducted largely in the open air, either in huge camp meetings as on the American frontier or in the open market squares of towns and villages as with Wesley and Whitefield in Britain.

As the churches spawned by the revival movements grew, they developed two very distinct worship services. One, usually in the morning, was clearly intended for those who were Christians. Smaller and stricter groups of churches reinforced the character of these 'believers meetings' by insisting that communion would be offered only to those who were known to be Christians. In my own denomination, within living memory, some chapels had wooden rails to separate those who were permitted to take communion from those who were not. Many such groups refused to accept money from those who were not church members and made sure that only the baptised could put money on the offering plate. Even today, in some of the farther reaches of the British Isles, one denomination at least does not publicise its communion service, partly as an attempt to ensure that only believers attend.

Although the strictures which surrounded the believers meetings were not common to the larger denominations, almost all churches of an evangelical persuasion held services which were designed for the unbeliever to attend. These were known as the gospel services and were usually held in the evening. Very often there was a conscious attempt to make the service attractive to the unbeliever. The service format was different to that of the morning and included rousing, contemporary hymns, special music items, testimony from those who had become Christians and gospel preaching designed to set forth the appeal of the Christian message.

As time went by and many churches lost something of their evangelistic cutting edge, fewer and fewer unbelievers attended these services. The gospel service often remained but more as a ritual than as a productive means of growth. The overwhelming majority of those who attended gradually came to consist almost entirely of the already converted. Some of the newer denominations at the end of the nineteenth century and the start of the twentieth century, such as the Salvation Army and then the Pentecostal groups, made significant attempts to utilise the concept of the gospel service. Today most of these attempts have taken on the same general pattern as the rest of the church.

The result has been that in many churches, both in Britain and America, services are held in the morning and in the evening with no clear idea of why Christians are expected to attend both. In the majority of churches where evening services still take place, it is only the really committed who turn up for the evening meeting.

As the clear distinction between a morning service for
believers and an evening service for unbelievers melted, there
has come a confusion, not only for the church but also for
those who still might be described as seekers. At one time in a
culture that was strongly influenced by the practice of church-
going, unbelievers and believers all knew which service they
were supposed to attend. But today unbelievers, or seekers,
are not aware of such a distinction. If they are inclined to
attend a church at all, it will almost certainly be the morning
service that they will come to. By and large the church is not
sure what to do with seekers at their regular service. On the
whole the language that is used, the hymns that are sung, the
messages that are preached are intended for believers.

In such a situation it is only the most determined seekers, or
those seekers who have been exposed to a church culture in the
past, that will be able to penetrate the mysteries offered in a
worship service intended for believers. So we arrive at the
situation where those with a burden for evangelism conclude
that a worship service would not be a good place for the
unbeliever to begin.

A more contemporary, if occasional, solution to such a
dilemma was the creation of the crusade meeting. Billy
Graham and others not so well known have produced a well-
developed formula explicitly designed to address the needs of
the unchurched. In essence, the Billy Graham team says to the
churches of a given locality, 'We will be coming to your area in
six months or a year's time. You cultivate relationships with
those you know to be unbelievers and invite them along to the
crusade. We in turn will produce a programme designed to
meet the needs of unbelievers. It will be different from your
regular services and we promise that it will be attractive to
those who never normally attend church.'

We should not underestimate the effectiveness of such an
approach. Research undertaken during the Mission England
and Mission to London crusades held by Billy Graham and
Luis Palau during 1984 and 1985 showed that some 65,000 of
those who made first-time decisions for Christ were attending
local churches one year after their initial decision to become a

Christian.[1] Such a total exceeds the entire membership of the Salvation Army or the Assemblies of God in Britain. But the problems of crusades are also well documented. Not all those who make decisions are able to make the transfer from football stadium to church sanctuary.

A course designed to help churches to welcome converts from the 1984 crusade of Billy Graham in Britain was entitled 'Is Your Church Worth Joining?'[2] We have to conclude that in many cases, converts answered that question by saying 'No'. In any case, even if every convert made the transition, crusades are by their very nature occasional events. One wonders what happens to those other potentially receptive 65,000 people who were not reached each year since 1985, simply because there have not been any crusades designed to meet their needs.

Bill Hybels has made an explicit connection between the approach of a Billy Graham crusade and the concept of the Seeker Service by describing it as being akin to having a Billy Graham meeting held every week in a local church. While this may be in some ways an oversimplification, nevertheless the Seeker Service framework does encapsulate many of the same principles that have been effectively used in the crusade approach. This is particularly true of the extent to which the event has a clear focus in terms of seeking to reach the unchurched with the gospel message, in a setting that is as helpful to those who are listening to the message as possible.

Some might argue that there is no real difference between the strategy of Willow Creek and the best use of the gospel service approach of earlier years. There is some truth in such a view. When I was a university student, I sometimes attended a church that had a very keen awareness of how to present an effective gospel service. The contrast with the church that I normally attended was so great as to be almost shocking. That particular church saw its evening gospel service attendance grow in a five-year period from less than 100 of its more faithful members to some 400 people, many of whom made commitments to Christ in that context.

So if some churches are able to run effective evening gospel services for the unchurched already, is there anything in the model developed by Willow Creek that can teach us something that we do not already know? Effective as some churches can be, there is a radicality and flexibility implied in the approach of Willow Creek. They have gone the extra step of saying that the needs of the unchurched must come first, so much so that everything that happens at a Sunday Seeker service is for unbelievers. Those who are potentially seeking for religious truth are not pushed into a single service, often held at a time so inconvenient that committed Christians can hardly be persuaded to come.

The needs of Christians are not ignored but the already committed are challenged to place such a high value on the needs of the unchurched that they are willing to be highly flexible as to the ways in which their own needs are met. Even in those churches that still run effective gospel services, there seems to be little appreciation of the extent of the cultural barrier that the unchurched have to cross. By dedicating themselves to understanding the extent of that gap, Willow Creek has produced a context for 'doing church' which requires both Christians and non-Christians to rethink the categories and assumptions that most people carry with them concerning their expectations of the church.

REMOVING THE BARRIERS

I had seen photographs of the Willow Creek facility before I ever arrived in Chicago. But driving towards the building across the 130 acres of landscaped campus, the building did not give quite the same impression as the few selected shots that I had seen. From a distance, the building looks more like a shopping mall than a church. Entering one of the many doors in the entrance system, a visitor comes into what looks like the foyer of a multiple screen movie complex. The huge entrance area is uncluttered with only a reception desk in the centre, dispensing directions instead of tickets. During services, television monitors relay the services in the foyer area. The carpeting is comfortable rather than sumptuous.

Entering the main auditorium is rather like visiting one of the newer provincial theatres in Britain, except that the seats at Willow Creek are more comfortable! There are no obvious religious images anywhere in the building. The front of the auditorium has a fairly conventional theatre-style stage. No communion table, cross, candles or pulpit are in sight. Each side of the auditorium features huge floor-to-ceiling tinted windows, set in aluminium frames.

The impact of the carefully maintained grounds and buildings is no accident. The first impression given to a seeker is considered to be very important. Willow Creek offers as its reason for such attention to detail the observation that:

> Seekers who come to Willow Creek Community Church are aware of every component of the church that they encounter. Looking for anything that will discredit what they are about to experience, the unbeliever scrutinizes all aspects of the church including the facility, the grounds and the actual service. For this reason, staff members and volunteers at Willow Creek Community Church are dedicated to excellence.[3]

Although I did not think about it consciously at the time, and although I was not looking to be critical in a hostile sense, I have to admit that I too was very aware of the surroundings that confronted me. Partly because of the desire to simply observe I arrived early for the service, and was able to watch the flow of traffic snaking down from one of the entrances into the main car parking area. My experience of working on the staff of a large church in North America during the 1970s meant that I was used to seeing a good amount of traffic movement, especially between services; but this was something very unusual. It was not just the number of vehicles visible at a glance, nor even the sense one had, when parking one's own car, of being very efficiently directed to a space. It was much more the feeling that there was no end to the number of vehicles that were arriving. This, and the large crowds of people in the foyer, quickly and quietly making their way to their seats, gave a sense of 'event'. Something was happening here; there was a feeling of expectation in the air.

It was very clear that all of those who were arriving felt very comfortable in these surroundings. The strategy that we spoke of in Chapter 3–of targetting a particular group–has been translated into the creation of an environment in which it is possible for the unchurched person to feel unthreatened. The gospel is being presented in a context familiar to those who work in modern office buildings, who are entertained in taste-ful theatres and whose homes have the same contemporary feel.

The degree of contextualisation marks this event out from a crusade meeting. The attendance at a crusade meeting is highly diverse in its composition and to some extent the con-tent of the meeting is a little hit-and-miss. Most crusades give some recognition to the fact that they are seeking to reach out to a highly diverse group by the inclusion of some evenings with a special emphasis, such as a youth evening, which have a slightly different programme content. There is very little which is hit-and-miss about the presentation at Willow Creek. The commitment to excellence is very evident.

Clearly, some Christians will be uncomfortable with such an approach. I suspect that because most Christians have a high level of integrity in the way in which they conduct their lives, there is always a worry about any presentation of the gospel that might contain an element of manipulation. Others might be concerned that the Christian message which is such an important part of the life of any sincere Christian is some-how being trivialised. We have already mentioned that Willow Creek has been accused of being in the entertainment busi-ness. It takes more than just attendance at one or two Seeker Services to answer such legitimate concerns, and we are right to constantly ask hard questions of any church group that is presenting a new approach to evangelism. However, it is also fair to ask to what extent Christians are able to imagine the magnitude of the barriers that the completely unchurched feel that they have to cross. The fact of the matter is that very few unchurched people are particularly anxious to attend a church of any description. Why then should the church make it harder for people to hear the gospel when they do come?

Bill Hybels illustrates this basic point by asking people to imagine that they have a Buddhist neighbour who invites them to attend the temple. If you were to accept such an invitation, it is very likely that the things that you would notice would be a combination of the physical surroundings and the warmth of welcome that you received. There is a very good possibility that the strangeness of the event would be so great that the actual belief structure that was part of the event would hardly penetrate your mind at all.

For a great many of the unchurched, the cultural barrier that needs to be crossed is just as great as that. The care and attention of Willow Creek to the detail of surroundings is not an attempt to water down the cost of becoming a Christian, it is simply an attempt to remove enough unnecessary barriers so that the Christian message can be given a fair hearing. The message of the cross contains a genuine and unavoidable offence by itself. There is no need for us to add to the offence of the gospel!

PROVIDING ANONYMITY

The experience of both crusade organisers and the pastors of larger churches that are successfully reaching the unchurched seems to be that those who are considering the claims of Christ prefer to be anonymous. This has nothing to do with a widespread Nicodemus syndrome in our society which would cause people to come at night! It is much more that the implications of the Christian message are far reaching enough for people to find it difficult enough to consider them without at the same time having to adjust to a whole new set of social relationships. A degree of anonymity provides some space for an unbeliever to do that kind of thinking.

The size of the event is part of the process of providing anonymity. Paradoxically, the majority of people who attend any church or evangelistic event do so because someone has invited them. You might well think that such an invitation removes the very anonymity that is so important. However, we need to remember that there is a significant difference between coping with an existing friendship that was sufficiently strong to allow someone to accept an invitation to attend, and the kind of exposure to many unknown people that happens when someone is asked to stand and identify themselves, and is then given a round of wild applause simply because they are a visitor.

The larger the event, the more possible it is for the person attending to become less aware of the person who brought them, even if they are sitting next to them. It is very hard to feel any degree of anonymity when sitting in a room with thirty other people, knowing that there is a very strong possibility that you are the only visitor there; and that the occasional – just slightly too long – glances in your direction suggest that your presence is producing a high degree of interest.

Anonymity is further enhanced by the quality of information that is made available to the visitor. Put very simply, the more a visitor knows what to expect, the less threatening the situation will be. Willow Creek takes great care that enough information is provided in the printed programme to meet this need. As the visitor comes into the auditorium he or she is handed a programme. This provides two kinds of information at a glance: what the major ingredients of the service are, and in what order they come. Information on the carefully selected activities of the church is also provided, much of which is also designed to meet the needs of those who are asking questions about the Christian faith.

Not only is great care taken to provide enough information in the programme to put the visitor at ease, attention is also paid to the layout of the programme, the quality of paper, print and design. The programme is not only an introduction to the church, it is probably the only physical reminder of the church that a visitor will take away. A visitor does not receive a hymnbook, prayer book, Bible or any other books or booklets which would only serve to confuse or distract a visitor as they begin to wonder how and when these other items will be used.

Those who crave anonymity do not want a high-profile

participation in the service. The nature of the participation that is asked for is therefore carefully thought through. There is very little congregational singing because non-churched people are generally unused to singing in public. When there is a song or hymn, hymnbooks are not required; the words appear in the programme, or on two large screens on either side of the auditorium. As with everything else at Willow Creek the projector slides are professionally presented, not handwritten with overhead projector pens! The songs are carefully chosen, not just in terms of their music content and overall relationship to the theme of the service. They have a contemporary feel and the words are chosen so that those who are singing them can do so with some integrity. Evangelical clichés are avoided.

No one is asked to identify themselves, to put up their hands, to sign anything or to volunteer for anything. The emphasis that is placed on the event is that the visitor is a guest and, as a guest, free to participate to the extent that they feel that they want to and no more.

Such a philosophy also extends to giving. An offering is taken but there is a careful and sensitive explanation indicating to visitors that since they are guests they can feel free not to contribute. There is no expectation that they should give. The approach to the offering is important, not only in terms of enhancing the tone of appropriate levels of participation but also as a response to the original research conducted by the church which indicated that the unchurched had a view of churches in general; that they were always asking for money.

Willow Creek estimate that in a group of some 12,500 people who attend on the weekend, possibly somewhere between 4,000 and 5,000 are uncommitted people who fall in the 'just looking' category. In a situation where there is an emphasis on non-participation, how do you help people to move on and yet preserve their anonymity? While the sermon that is preached does not press for decisions, in that no altar call is made, nevertheless the underlying ethos of the spoken message and indeed of the whole service is that it does challenge people to make a response, even if that response is only to begin to think. Willow Creek firmly leaves the initiative with the seeker.

The church does provide assistance. The programme contains a section where people may ask for more information, although once again there is a promise that no one from the church will visit unless they are requested to do so. Further information is also available at strategic points in the building as people enter and leave, but seeking information is always left to the seeker's initiative. Clearly there is an expectation that those who invited the visitor will have a conversation with their guest. The question of what their friend thought of the service, of the church and of the message will certainly arise, but not in a manner which will put premature pressure on the individual to make a commitment. The hope and expectation of the church is that those who come for a first visit will come again. The sermons often follow a series theme which helps to encourage further visits to hear the rest of the series.

TIME TO DECIDE

The strategy of the church to encourage further visits is critical. It is not because those at the church are such pleasant and mild-manner people that they would regard asking anyone for a decision as offensive to good taste; there is a realisation that when it comes to teaching the unchurched, time is a critical ingredient. Willow Creek estimates that it typically takes six to twelve months of attendance before someone who is unchurched is in a position to make any kind of decision. In some cases the time required will be greater.

Why should such a time interval be required? Three factors are apparent:

1. The search for meaning

It has been observed by many in the field of evangelism that there are times of particular openness to the gospel. Those times of openness fall broadly into two categories. The first is that of *crisis*. Any traumatic event, the sudden and unexpected death of a loved one, the news of one's own impending death, the sudden loss of employment and status, the breakdown of significant relationships–these and other life-threatening or life-changing events can cause people to dramatically reassess their priorities, lifestyles and values. Sometimes such a re-evaluation lasts no longer than the immediate crisis; once a new equilibrium is established large issues tend to be ignored and previous values reassert themselves.

Clearly those who are involved in helping people at times of crisis have a huge responsibility not to use such events to manipulate people at a time of great vulnerability. Nevertheless, it is the case that sometimes crisis events do lead to genuine and long-lasting faith commitments.

The second type of openness is also often related to the theme of *change* and might be described simply as the quest for meaning. Often, it is the less immediate points of crisis induced by the well-known stages in the life cycle that help to raise this question. Puberty, marriage, the arrival of one's own children, the mid-life crisis, retirement and the increasing awareness of the mortality of others (and so by implication of oneself) are all points at which issues relating to meaning tend to be raised.[4]

Although of course there are those who come to Willow Creek as a result of a significant and immediate crisis, the orientation of the church (and one suspects its most effective evangelistic outreach) is towards those who fall in the category of those who are searching for meaning. Unlike the search for an answer to an immediate crisis which can often be met by an experience of sudden conversion, the search for meaning usually takes longer. Time and space to think through such issues are important ingredients in helping an individual through such a process.

2. The implications of such a decision

The preaching and ethos of Willow Creek make it very clear that a decision to become a Christian is not an insignificant matter. It is very obvious simply by the care and attention to detail which has gone into the creation of a Seeker Service that these people believe something, and that they consider it important enough to want to put a great deal of effort into communicating it, no matter how sensitively, to others. It therefore follows that to begin to believe the same things, to become a Christian, will not be a part-time activity, an added extra which like aerobics one can do at certain hours without it inconveniencing the rest of life.

The decision to become a Christian will affect one's marriage partner and children, finances, business life, lifestyle, friendships, priorities and values. Those who come to Willow Creek as seekers are often people who have to make significant decisions in other areas of their life and they do not make far-reaching decisions lightly. Nor should they. The scripture makes it clear that 'counting the cost' is something that every potential disciple should engage in before making a commitment. Such evaluation takes time.

3. A paradigm shift

For those who have been nurtured in a world which operates on the basis of a secular world view, the conceptual distance which has to be travelled between such a view and the possibility of Christian faith is considerable. James Engel has attempted to describe and document the various stages or processes that a person passes through in order to embrace the Christian faith. His work has become known as the Engel scale. There are a considerable number of stages on such a scale through which a seeker passes before there comes any kind of active consideration of the claims of the Christian faith.

Engel devised his scale in the far East, in the context of a culture which was largely hostile to Christianity but not hostile to religious faith. His scale does not really have any way of taking into account the degree of hostility towards the validity of any religious faith that is engendered by our secular culture. Anyone who is concerned to share the Christian message must take account of the impact of secularism, which tends to mean that the very presuppositions upon which people base their lives already rule out the possibility of the Christian message being true.

The means by which such a situation has arisen in our culture is complex, and this is not the place to describe such a process in detail. However we can obtain a brief sketch of the real impact of such a process by looking at the fields of education and media, areas of activity which, when taken together, exercise a considerable influence on what people believe about the world around them. Various studies have shown that exposure to a secular scientific world view has a dramatic influence on the lives of young people, producing a considerable change in their views between the ages of eleven and fourteen. Writing about the impact of education on young people, a British educationalist cites research on this matter and comments:

> Moderate hedonism, individualism and insistence on open-mindedness were among the key aspects that emerged in some research conducted in 1977 on young people's beliefs. 'A strong dislike of having other people's beliefs pushed on you' was particularly noted. Their own beliefs seemed superficial, consumerist, and pragmatic, tinged with some fascination with the occult. They put their faith in facts and a simplistic scientism, and they saw no point in trying to reflect on a consistent and well founded philosophy of life. Religion took up no part of their world.[5]

The influences that shape our world view as teenagers tend to be reinforced by the all-persuasive views of the media as adulthood replaces adolescent experiences. A British broadcaster, noting the well-known phrase of Marshall McLuhan, 'The medium is the message', takes up a lesser-known phrase by the same commentator: 'The medium is the massage'.

While people may be sharply aware of the content of television programmes or of newspaper stories, for example, they are rarely aware of how much time they actually spend in absorbing media messages. McLuhan's point is that we have allowed the mass media to 'massage' us into a state of unreflecting and indiscriminating cultural consumption.[6]

The influence of media, whether print, audio or visual, operates at what has been called the 'broadcasting' and the 'narrowcasting' levels. The media contributes at a broadcast level helping to reinforce the broadly secular perspective of our society. I recently spent time talking to a television producer who normally works in current affairs but who tries to persuade his superiors in one of the leading television companies in Britain to allocate funding for religious programming. Inevitably he is greeted with the argument that the company concerned has to take the potential size of audience into account before allocating any funds to any project. There is considerable evidence to indicate that the audiences for religious programming are very high. The producer in question claimed that when faced with this objective evidence, those who make the financial decisions completely discount such facts. What counts for them is that they do not know anyone who is interested in religion, especially Christianity. It is therefore considered to be unimportant, at best marginal, and, no matter how large the actual viewing audience, not what a good television company should be doing.

Thus, what appears on our screens is inevitably filtered by those who were at university twenty years ago and who were therefore being influenced by the dominant secular views of their own professors. By now these are very old ideas, many of which are academically discredited; but discredited or not, they still help to shape our culture at a very broad level.

Besides this broad level of influence, there is also what has been called narrowcasting. This is an attempt by media to respond to the various segmented interests of our society. So, in Britain, the subcultures inhabited by readers of the national newspapers, the *Guardian* and the *Sun*, represent two very different worlds, worlds which in many respects scarcely overlap. Very few people would read both the *Sun* and the *Guardian*. The increasing specialisation of the media whether as cable television or specialist magazine produces a tendency

towards a fragmentation into what one writer has called 'mutually unintelligible cultural worlds'.[7] The point about many of
these worlds is that Christianity is specifically excluded.

To move from such a world—or in the case of narrowcasting, worlds—to the world of the Bible and Christian faith
requires what many writers have called a 'paradigm shift'.
Such a shift means the replacement of one set of ideas with a
completely different set. A paradigm shift only takes place
when an existing set of ideas no longer fits the experience of a
person's life to such an extent that a revolution in thinking
becomes necessary. Usually it takes time to make a paradigm
shift.

The strategy of the Seeker Service is to provide a venue
which is sufficiently close to the language and forms of the
surrounding culture that the inbuilt hostility of our culture to
any kind of faith can be temporarily reduced while a consideration of the Christian message takes place. Although, as we
have said, paradigm shifts take time, Willow Creek demonstrates that they can take place on a significant scale.

FOOTNOTES

1. Detailed research on the Mission Crusades in 1984 was conducted by Gallup on behalf of Bible Society. Additional research on what happened to the converts from Mission to London was conducted by Linda Barley of Bible Society.

2. This course was an adaptation of the Bible Society's course 'What Makes Churches Grow?', which is still available to churches.

3. This quotation is taken from a document published by Willow Creek and entitled *Overview*.

4. For a longer discussion of this issue in the context of evangelism see M. Robinson and S. Christine, *Planting Tomorrow's Churches Today* (Monarch: 1992), pp 284, 299f.

5. Brenda Watson, 'Education and the Gospel', in Hugh Montefiore (ed), *The Gospel and Contemporary Culture* (SPCK: 1992), p 136.

6. Jim McDonnell, 'Mass Media, British culture and Gospel values', in *ibid*, p 160.

7. *Ibid*, p 161.

CHAPTER FIVE

The Ingredients
of a Seeker Service

T HE NINETEENTH CENTURY, both in Britain and America, represented a high-water mark for the sermon as a form of popular entertainment. Legendary tales are told of how preachers would sometimes place an hour glass on the pulpit. When the glass was completely empty and the preacher was coming to a close, the more popular preachers were reputedly urged to turn the hour glass over to great cheers of appreciation from the crowd. It is difficult to imagine such a scene taking place today, no matter how gifted the preacher!

This change in the role of preaching in our society is not just a reflection of the changing position of the church in our society. It is part of a much more complex web of changes that have comprehensively affected social patterns. The effect of these changes has often been to isolate the church from the mainstream of cultural expression in our society, forcing the church to communicate across an increasingly significant cultural chasm.

Writing on the subject of communication across cultures, David Hesselgrave and Edward Rommen offer a seven-dimension grid by which to try and understand the ingredients in cross-cultural communication. The various elements in their grid are all critical in terms of understanding the process of contextualising the gospel for particular cultural groups. However, the most important ingredient in terms of understanding the significance of the Seeker Service strategy is the step that they describe as 'Media influence—ways of channeling communication'.

Hesselgrave and Rommen refer to Marshall McLuhan's classic phrase which we have already quoted: 'The medium is the message'.[1] In other words, whether we like it or not, the way in which we choose to communicate significantly affects what people hear of our message. There is no 'pure' form of communication that allows people to hear exactly what we intend to communicate. A variety of filters act to subtly change our message until it may be unrecognisable to us.

The form of our communication of the gospel or 'good news' has often meant that many people hear our message as a burden or as something which is far from good; and because they think that they have heard it so many times before, it ceases to be news. What kind of gospel are we preaching that is neither 'good' nor 'news'?[2]

breathreHow then can we communicate that, despite the distortions of the past, the gospel is in fact good news? Two factors are crucial. First, we must use those forms of communication which are a common currency in the mainstream of our culture, and through which people receive most of the important messages that already influence and shape their lives. Second, it is vital to use a variety of those communication forms, so that the message is communicated on a number of levels, each level acting to reinforce the others.

THE USE OF MUSIC

Today, popular forms of music resonate through our culture as never before. The phrases associated with particular songs become interwoven within our culture and conjure up all kinds of images ranging from sentimentality to violence. Advertising is dominated by the 'jingle' and the most popular radio stations play non-stop music. A single phrase, 'She loves you, yeah, yeah, yeah', designates a whole generation.

Some sections of the church have a reputation for excellence in the presentation of music. Unfortunately, the music that we speak of is music that constitutes a minority interest. Wonderful as *Messiah* is, such music does not form a large part of the popular diet of music that influences so strongly the messages that many in our culture breathe in every day. At this point, life becomes complicated. Clearly, there is no single form of popular music. Even among teenagers, what communicates to one group does not communicate to another. Heavy metal has little in common with the current revival of interest in artists from the 1960s; hip-hop and rap are far different from pop or blues.

The precise choice of musical style is critically important. It is essential to think hard about the target audience when selecting the musical style of the church. What music do they like? It is vital that we are not too influenced by our own musical tastes. The staff of Willow Creek frequently joke that if the music programme of the church were to be decided on the basis of Bill Hybels' taste, then the entire programme would consist of country and western music, which is a long way from being the preferred music of the group that Willow Creek tries to reach.

Having decided on the overall musical style that would be appropriate, the next question is much simpler but also harder to answer: Where does one find appropriate material? Surprising as it may seem to musical philistines such as myself, it does exist in surprising quantities, but you often have to look quite hard for it. There is a huge range of Christian material available in recorded form and although only a small proportion of it is suitable for presentation in the context of a Seeker Service, it is possible to find enough material if you sift for long enough. Nor is there any need to be limited to specifically Christian lyrics. Some of the most powerful songs used by Willow Creek are in fact secular songs, but ones that ask profound questions about the meaning and direction of life.

However, whether choosing secular or Christian songs, it is hard work to constantly come up with good material.

A further problem revolves around the issue of the level of talent that is required to perform adequately even the best of material. A good song played badly fails utterly to communicate on a significant level. Worse than that, the message of the gospel is easily compromised by a poor performance. Whether we like it or not, all those whom we seek to attract have access through television to the very best of entertainment standards and have come to expect that level of performance to typify whatever they see. We will be judged more against the standard of television performers than by what their immediate neighbours might be able to produce. It is essential to select those who are competent to perform and who are willing to dedicate the time to making this a real ministry. It is emphatically *not* just a matter of sticking in a song to pad out the programme. The music is a vital ingredient in the communication process; adequate rehearsal time is both necessary and vital.

A further difficult issue arises as the size of event grows. The bigger the church, the more likely it is that fresh talent will emerge from those who come. It is also true that the bigger the event, the greater will be the demand in terms of the level of ability that is required to make communication effective. In short, those who performed very well to a group of 100 may well be the wrong people to sing and play to a group of 500. Handling the necessary transition of personnel requires great pastoral skill and a commitment to use those who have served faithfully in the past in alternative ministries which are equally satisfying.

THE INGREDIENT OF DRAMA

Much of what has already been said about music could be repeated in the context of a drama presentation. The necessity for quality and the commitment of time and energy on the part of those who seek to make this a ministry, are all just as important for drama as they are for music.

To some extent, we are helped by the expectations aroused by secular culture because the emphasis of the professional theatre (with the exception of musicals) has not been on elaborate sets. A great deal of drama has featured the minimum of special costumes and stage setting, concentrating instead on simple props. The essential ingredient is that the sketch, which need be no more than ten minutes long, should portray a situation with which the audience can easily identify.

Drama does not seek to preach a message in the sense of always giving solutions. Still less is drama used to make a complete presentation of the gospel message. The heart of drama is to present a dilemma, to dramatise the questions that are present in the lives of those in the audience. The best drama will cause people to ask questions about their own situation as a result of identifying with the actors on stage. 'They could have been talking about me,' is the response that a good drama produces.

Where does one obtain that kind of material? Again it does exist, coming both from secular and Christian writers. However, those who are considering introducing a Seeker Service approach today at least have the advantage of the more than fifteen years' experience of Willow Creek. A great deal of the material used by Willow Creek is available in published form.

However, be cautious! Do not think that because it has worked for Willow Creek in that precise form it somehow has a kind of magic, which—although it is not evident to you just by reading the words—clearly *must* be there because Willow Creek is a growing church. 'This sketch must work,' you tell yourself, as you slavishly rehearse the material just as it is printed in the book. Remember that the precise formulation of the material is highly contextualised. It may well be that the best use of the Willow Creek drama material for you may just be to stimulate your own creativity. It would be surprising, not to say incredible, if no adaptation of material were to take place.

MULTI-MEDIA PRESENTATIONS

As early as the Son City days, the concept of using multi-media presentations to communicate the message became part of the Willow Creek approach. In essence, multi-media presentations make use of sound and image projection to put together a series of visual and audio messages. In effect, we watch multi-media presentations every time we watch advertising on television.

Advertising is not so much a reasoned presentation of a set of objective facts as the communication of a series of bite-sized messages, each of which is designed to leave a feeling or an impression of the product with the potential purchaser. Much the same kind of presentation accompanies pop songs on channels such as MTV. Again, it is an important medium by which many messages are given and received in our culture. An older formulation of the same principle is summed up in the tradition of photo-journalism: 'One good picture is worth a thousand words'.

In the Willow Creek context, one form of multi-media presentation is the use of a cartoon-type character which speaks, although the 'words' are simply sounds which cannot be understood by those watching. The message is conveyed visually and primarily through humour, as the figure on the screen attempts to solve the dilemma that he finds himself in.

Again, not an easy thing to do well; but there are other ways of using projected images to help convey a message. It may well be that you have access to short film clips, or even to still slides which can creatively convey a message. It is important to use the medium itself to communicate and not attempt to overlay it in some way just to make sure that the point is taken. Often we are so obsessed by words that we can have a very beautiful piece of film and then so dominate it with commentary that we might just as well not have used film at all. Far too many Christian videos have made this mistake and have ended up going down the 'talking heads' route, thereby undermining the very nature of the visual media that is being used.

It is also important for multi-media presentations to be short. It is only necessary to communicate one simple message in a few minutes. Anything too complex or too long puts too much weight on the medium. Its main purpose is to reinforce the message that is being conveyed by other means. It is not a substitute for preaching.

THE SCRIPTURE READING

It would be unthinkable for anyone to suggest that we should not read the Bible in a church service. However, most of those who preach are only too aware that few if any members of a congregation can remember the passage that has been read with any degree of accuracy. Some churches attempt to reduce the problem by having pew Bibles available, so that the congregation can follow along. Other churches will read the passage responsively or in some other dramatic fashion, trying to ensure that the content is communicated.

One theologian who is deeply concerned for the place of the Bible in our culture has commented that even in evangelical churches the Bible is often used as an ikon.[3] In other words, we like to have the Bible read and preached from, but it does not really constitute an authoritative revelation which Christians actually use as a basis for decision-making in their daily lives. Surveys show that the level of Bible ignorance even amongst evangelical Christians is serious and getting worse.[4]

Still less can we expect the unchurched person to come to our church ready to listen and relate strongly to the public reading of Scripture. Nevertheless, it is vital that we begin the task of restoring the credibility of the Bible, whether or not those who are coming to our church as visitors accept its authority as a starting point.

Bible readings at Willow Creek are usually fairly short. Before they are read, the reader (usually a member of the ministry staff) tells a personal story or describes a current event which relates to the fundamental theme of the passage. The intention is to help to reinforce the relevance of the passage for today's world.

THE ANNOUNCEMENTS AND THE OFFERING

The focus for the announcements that are given each week is the Seeker. Those who are church members and who need to receive information relevant to the church programme are given that information either in the programme or at the mid-week New Community Service. The purpose of the announcement section in the Seeker Service is only to give a welcome to those who have come, to draw attention to the places where those who are seekers can obtain further information or involvement should they desire it, and to act as a smooth transition to the offering time.

As indicated in the previous chapter, visitors are told that they do not need to participate in this part of the service. Clearly, it is very important that this information should be conveyed in the right way. A poor presentation could well result in giving as much offence at not inviting people to participate, as it would if a newcomer felt he was being pressured to give.

THE MESSAGE

In more recent times, the preaching at Willow Creek has been the responsibility of a team of four of which Bill Hybels is just one team member; but it has become strongly identified with Hybels' preaching style and person. As one Chicago area newspaper put it in a headline, 'Why do 12,000 people a week flock to hear what this man has to say?'[5]

When Bill Hybels stands up to preach, he speaks from a plexiglass lectern. As Elmer Towns puts it: 'Hybels, in a business suit, looks less like a clergyman than an executive commuting to the Chicago loop.'[6] The issues, illustrations, the slang and particularly the humour relate strongly to the kind of person who would be travelling to the Chicago Loop. The sermon lasts for some 35-40 minutes, which although a little long in a British context and even for most US churches, seems to be an acceptable presentation-length in this context.

Although it is true that people return to Willow Creek as a result of the total experience, the environment, the music and the drama, it is difficult to avoid the conclusion that the message is the most critical part of the package even if it is only measured in terms of time. The sermon takes up more than half of the one hour and ten minutes service time. So what are the features that strengthen the preaching of Hybel and his team?

First, a vital ingredient of both the sermon and the total event is the degree to which there is a critique of each service after the occasion. The point of the critique is not to make the preacher feel either good or bad, so much as to allow the person to consistently improve their performance through constructive criticism. That sounds like a good idea that ought to work in any situation. However, when you try it, you will be amazed at how few people, including yourself, can cope with such a process. Strong team relationships and a healthy self-image are essential qualifications for being able to engage in such an exercise.

Second, preaching to the unchurched in this kind of way is hard work! It is far easier to preach to Christians, not only because as Christians ourselves we know our audience somewhat better than we know those who are unchurched. The whole orientation of clergy training, the tradition of which we are a part and possibly even of the expectations of our existing congregation do not equip us for such a task. It is hard work to constantly discover what is on the mind of the unchurched. It is hard work to come up with the factual information that we will need for the sermon; it is hard work to come up with illustrations from everyday life, instead of from the life of Martin Luther or St Paul or in fact anybody who lived before the beginning of the twentieth century.

Third, thematic or issue-based preaching, especially in the form of a series, is helpful in terms of attempting to meet the needs of those who attend. It is interesting to note the number of times that the sermons at Willow Creek touch on issues related to family life–improving your marriage, being a better husband, enriching family life; these and other similar themes are valuable because marriages and family life are under increasing pressure. Monogamy is increasingly seen as a serial matter rather than as a lifetime commitment—only one wife at a time! The attraction of a sermon can be enhanced through its title. 'You matter to God' is one example of an effective title for a Seeker Service message. You may not like it but for the unchurched person it communicates far more than 'The cleansing of the Temple', for which it would be a very good substitute! Bill Hybels tells of a sermon series which he preached which, in terms of content was, according to the elders, one of the best sermon series that he ever preached to the unchurched. But the title of the series—'A portrait of Jesus'—was not attractive to unchurched people and the attendance for that series declined.

Fourth, preaching to challenge. We noted in the previous chapter that most of the sermons are not intended to lead to an immediate decision in the sense of issuing an altar call. The major aim of the sermon is to challenge people to think, to take the claims of the Christian faith seriously and to see how they apply in the various areas of life.

However there are some occasions, often at the conclusion of a series, when people are challenged to make a decision. Such a challenge would take a variety of forms. People might be asked to put up their hands if they have made some kind of commitment (this happens rarely); they might be asked to pray silently and then to indicate to someone after the service that they have made a commitment; or they might be encouraged to come and pray with the preacher after the service has finished.

Fifth, the strategy of demonstrating the application of the Bible. If I were to single out one aspect of the preaching at the Seeker Service that is significantly different from most preaching to Christian audiences, it would be this ingredient. Bill Hybels is a master at being able to say to people: 'This is what the Bible says on a given subject: even if you aren't a Christian, these principles will work, so give them a try.' Frankly, there are very few sermons that I ever hear elsewhere that are sufficiently practical in their content to be able to make such a connection.

What I have just described is, in effect, the practical apologetic that Willow Creek has developed in its dialogue with secularised people. It is sometimes said that Christians know that Jesus is the answer but they have forgotten the question. The importance of Willow Creek's practical apologetic is that it attempts to answer the question that our secular society asks. What is that question?

At one time, the most important question in our society was the question, 'Is it true?' That is the question that most Christian apologetics are designed to answer. 'Is it true that Jesus rose from the dead?', 'Is the Bible accurate?' and so on. However, the impact of secularism is such that many no longer ask the question 'Is it true?' in the field of morals or faith. It is assumed that since all faith and morality are firmly in the area of opinion and that all opinions are equally valid, the only thing that really matters is whether or not they work: 'Does it work?' is the question that arises again and again. Never mind if the suggested formula is derived from Hinduism, Buddhism, the occult or Christianity—the main question asked is 'Does it work?'. Bill Hybels answers that question directly by saying, 'Christianity *does* work; even if you can't yet accept the whole package, try this particular principle and see if it works...'

From here Hybels goes on in effect to show that the reason that Christianity works is that it is true. This process is essential if people are going to be able to make the paradigm shift that we spoke of in the previous chapter. The jump from a secular world view to a Christian world view, in which the Bible is accepted as an authentic and true revelation, is too great to make in one step. The vital stepping stone is the intermediate step of the applicability of the message.

Interestingly, the approach of Willow Creek is often contrasted with that of John Wimber and the Vineyard Fellowship which stresses the importance of signs and wonders. Although the model is different, the methodology is remarkably similar. Both men are committed to answering the same fundamental question of our culture—'Does it work?'—as part of an apologetic that seeks to move people to a new biblical paradigm. Wimber seeks to do this through a demonstration in signs and wonders that Christianity works and is therefore true, while Hybels and Willow Creek seek another form of practical demonstration. At least in their ultimate goals, the two may not be as far apart as some suppose. Indeed it could also be argued that both approaches represent an appropriate contextualisation of their method, given the location of Wimber in California and Willow Creek in corporate Chicago.

MAKING THE PROGRAMME WORK

No matter how gifted the musicians, the actors and the preacher; no matter how creative the multi-media presentation; unless the ingredients of the service are properly managed, then the overall effect may be far from impressive. At Willow Creek, Nancy Beach acts as the programme director whose responsibility it is to integrate the various parts of the service, much as a theatre producer would be responsible for the overall direction of a play or similar production. It is helpful if one person can be assigned such a responsibility without also having to carry a major role in any other part of the programme. The skills that are needed to pull the programme together are specialised and call for someone to be trained, either on the job or in some other way. Key areas to be aware of are as follows.

First, the items in each service need to centre on an agreed theme so that every ingredient serves to support the message that will be presented in the sermon. This is an obvious point, but it requires team discussion well before the event.

Second, the links between each item need to be well thought through. It is all too easy for the impact of each part of the event to be lost in a clumsy transition from one item to the next.

Third, the pace of the service needs to be maintained or it can become somewhat slow and tedious. In this context it is important to make sure that each item is carefully timed so that the whole event is the right length. Failure to achieve proper timing puts pressure on the most important part of the service, the message. It is obviously counterproductive to have a high degree of excellence in the drama and music pieces only for them to run over time and so detract from the message.

The technical aspects of the production require careful thought. Good sound and lighting are essential in giving a professional feel to a Seekers Service. This requires substantial investment in high-quality equipment and training in using it properly. Attention to detail is vital. For example, it is astonishing what impact lighting adds to the perceived interest of the speaker. One would perhaps imagine that a speaker needs only a good sound system, but in fact lighting also serves to enhance the degree to which an audience can concentrate on what a speaker is saying. This kind of expertise needs to be developed by observing what those in the professional theatre do and then experimenting to achieve the appropriate presentation with the facilities that you have at your disposal.

ANOTHER TIME, ANOTHER PLACE

When Willow Creek's leaders made the transition from Son City to an event targetted for adults, they moved the event from a mid-week session to a Sunday morning. They did so because of a perception that in the culture that they were seeking to reach the most likely time that a seeker would think of attending church would be on a Sunday morning. the current format comprises two services on a Saturday evening and two on a Sunday morning. These events are held at these times because it is believed that these are the most likely times that seekers in that area would attend. There is no Sunday evening service because of a perception that the target audience would not respond at that time. The ethos of the event and the precise ingredients are all tailored to the audience that is being targetted.

But Willow Creek began with an effective ministry to youth, and frankly one does not see many young people in the weekend seeker services. This is because on Tuesday evenings Willow Creek moves to a different beat. Not only is it a stronger beat but the audio visuals are much more radical. If any adults were to inadvertently wander in, they might be excused for thinking that they were attending a pop concert. Loud whoops of excitement add to the sense of high energy that vibrates through the hall. The 1,500 young people have not been dragged along by their parents. This is clearly the best place to be on a Tuesday evening. This is Son City, recreated for the 1990s and renamed 'Student Impact'.

There is a very different feel to all that takes place. The basic ingredients of a music, drama, audio-visual presentation and a challenging message are all there; but the cultural clothes in which they are presented are very different. Inevitably, every Seeker Service has to be contextualised. There may be some locations in Britain where the precise model of Willow Creek would work exactly as it stands with only the accents changed. There will be many places, both in America and in Britain, where the ingredients would be the same. But the way in which they would be presented would need to be very different.

How does one know what precise format would work? What time of day or day of the week would be best for a seeker service in another locality? How does one go about finding the answer to such questions? The most basic response is to encourage each group that is considering a Seeker Service strategy to engage in research to find the answers to such questions.

It is all too tempting for church leaders who have seen Willow Creek to go home, train up their people, order materials from Willow Creek and then duplicate as closely as possible what they have seen there. That might work, but the key factor in determining whether or not it will do so will not be the degree of professionalism in the presentation, but the fit of the programme to your culture and whether or not those in your church will invite others to come.

It may be that you have a congregation that does not have many significant friendships with those who are not Christians. If that is so, not only are you not ready to hold a Seeker Service, but you will not have the access to the most vital piece of information that you need in order to stage one. In order to conduct research so that you can answer key questions as to the time and format of the event, it is essential to ask the views of those people who you anticipate will come. When would they come? What format would they find most comfortable? What music do they like? And most important of all, what are they thinking, what issues are on their mind?

It is not enough just to put on a Seeker Service, no matter how well presented, and then to sit back and hope that people will come on their own. They almost certainly will not. Finding a church service to attend is not a high priority on most people's weekend list of activities. The most essential key of all to the success of a Seeker Service lies with the friendships that your people have or don't yet have with the unchurched.

FOOTNOTES

1. David Hesselgrave and Edward Rommen, *Contextualization: Meanings, Methods and Models* (Apollos: 1989), p 208.

2. Walter Hollenweger discusses this issue further in his book, *Evangelism Today: Good News or Bone of Contention?* (CJL: 1976).

3. Dan Beeby has made this point in a so far unpublished paper, 'Recovering Scripture' (February 1991).

4. 'Attitudes to the Bible, God and Church'—research commissioned by Bible Society and conducted by Gallup in 1983—revealed that 35% of adults had never read the Bible at all and a further 23% had never read it regularly at any time in their lives. Moreover, the younger the person the less likely they were to have read the Bible, thus producing a trend towards greater Bible ignorance. The survey showed that more than half of the adult population do not know the content of the Gospels.

5. The headline in the *Daily Herald*, Suburban Living section, 18 May, 1988.

6. Elmer towns, *10 of Today's Most Innovative Churches* (Regal: 1990), p 44.

CHAPTER SIX

An Evangelistic Heart

THE CLEAR FOCUS of Willow Creek Community Church has been to win the unchurched to Christ. For the leaders at Willow Creek, that has meant investing all that they are and all that they have in developing the life and witness of their own congregation. They have not been involved in winning people to Christ through church planting. It is solely because they are convinced that their mandate up to this point has been to work with Willow Creek. However, the influence of their witness has spread to other parts of North America and to other parts of the world as visitors have come to observe, learn and apply their insights to other situations. That learning process has been deliberately fostered through the sponsorship of leadership conferences held three times a year at Willow Creek.

The leaders have commented that it has not been unusual for other congregations to establish a Seeker Service organised on a similar pattern to that of Willow Creek, only to conclude after three or six months that it didn't work for them. On closer inspection, it often turns out that the difficulties inherent in using such a strategy were not fully understood before the attempt was made. The experience of those who have attempted to implement a Seeker Service strategy clearly indicates that while the unchurched are receptive to such an approach, existing church members have a great deal of difficulty in making such a transition.

The dilemma for an existing church is simply this: a service intended for unbelievers does not meet the needs of those who are Christians. Even so, many Christians can be persuaded to attend an event intended primarily for unbelievers if they see large numbers of unbelievers attending and becoming Christians. However, in the early stages of a transition, there is often a 'wait and see' factor. Usually there will be a minority of Christians in a congregation who have enough unchurched friends for them to be able to give invitations. Even these few will usually want to wait and see whether the event maintains a consistently high quality before inviting those friends. Since it is also true that even when the unchurched do come they will not in most cases make a decision to become a Christian for some time, there is a considerable period when it appears that nothing significant is taking place.

It is very possible for there to be a build-up of frustration among the Christians in the congregation. In effect some will be saying to themselves, 'We are putting ourselves out to attend an event which isn't meeting our needs and there does not seem to be any tangible benefit.' It is not unheard of for Seeker Service strategies to fall apart at this point. For this reason, the leaders at Willow Creek have observed that the creation of a Seeker Service strategy often works best in a new church situation.

But even in a new church situation it is vital to stress that the core group of Christians needs training if a service, designed to meet needs of seekers, is to take off. Yet that seems strange. Why would it be necessary to train church members to invite others to come to something that was clearly excellent? Wouldn't it be the case that if a programme were good enough, church members would be certain to invite their friends along? In an ideal world that might be true, but experience shows that while Christians usually agree about the importance of evangelism and outreach, actually doing it is more problematic. I was struck recently by the words of a

Romanian church leader, Professor Otniel Bunaciu, who said to his fellow Christians, 'We have been speaking for fifty years about mission and evangelism. But now that we have the freedom to do it, we don't.'[1] He might well have been speaking for the whole church!

The covenant that Willow Creek has made with its members therefore has two parts. The first is the part we have already noted, that if church members will invite their friends, Willow Creek will provide a presentation of the gospel that will be sufficiently excellent for no Christian to be embarrassed to invite any of their friends. The second part of that covenant is just as important: namely that the church will help train them to do just that.

The conviction that every member of the church will be involved in the evangelistic process is central to the evangelistic philosophy at Willow Creek, so much so that out of an approximate annual budget of $10,000,000 only about $25,000, or one quarter of one percent of budget, is set aside for advertising and promotion. Almost all of this sum is used to enhance the process of personal invitation that lies at the centre of Willow Creek's life. Occasionally, large newspaper advertisements are placed, not on the extensive church notices page but in the entertainments section. The purpose of these advertisements is to act as a talking point for church members in their conversations with people. Much of the rest of the budget is spent on personal invitation cards for special events, again designed to assist the strategy of personal invitation.

BUILDING AUTHENTIC RELATIONSHIPS

No matter what data one considers—whether it be the biblical record, the analysis of those who respond to Billy Graham missions in Western countries, or the more informal soundings of those who have become Christians in countries such as Russia or China—it is clear that the overwhelming number of conversions to Christianity have taken place through the influence of someone who was known and trusted by that person. Such an insight is hardly remarkable, and in some ways is perhaps reassuring. Despite all the sophistication of a highly technological age, the commendation of any idea, product or innovation carries considerably more credibility if it is recommended by someone we trust.

Bill Hybels uses the illustration of his own experience in declining to read a piece of literature handed to him by a stranger at an airport because he didn't feel that he had time to read it, whereas he did read a whole book because it was sent to him by someone he knew and respected. The lesson is obvious. It is essential for us to cultivate friendships with the unchurched if we want them to take our message seriously.

As we have noted, Christians tend not to have many significant relationships with the unchurched. I can well remember the sense of shock that I experienced early in my ministry because I met so many men who worked on the industrial shop floor who told me candidly that they had never met a Christian before. Very probably there were some Christians at their workplace who had never found an opportunity to speak about their faith, but when it came to the sphere of social life, many of these men were absolutely sure that they had never met a single Christian. It is perhaps hardly surprising. Not only would few Christians feel able to share in some of the social activities of some of the men that I have in mind, but in any case our church life, especially in resource-starved smaller congregations, hardly allows any time for family life, let alone for social involvement with the unchurched.

But how can anyone train us to build authentic relationships with others? In one sense any attempt to train people to build authentic relationships is a contradiction in terms. For any relationship to be authentic it needs to be one that is formed naturally and not on the basis of a training package! However, that does not mean that we can do nothing as churches to encourage Christians to form such relationships.

The one thing that leaders can do is practice what they preach! David Schmidt is a Consultant in strategic planning, marketing and development who worships at Willow Creek and also advises a number of churches on their programmes. During one of my visits to Willow Creek, David told me of a conversation that he had had with Bill Hybels not long after he had started to attend the church. Bill, having heard of David's work with churches, asked him, 'How many people have you led to Christ recently?' David responded, 'You don't understand: I train others to lead people to Christ.' But Bill Hybels kept coming back to him, challenging him to put into practice the things that he was teaching.

That story made a considerable impact on me, since I was in very much the same position as David Schmidt. It is my job to write on mission, to train others in mission and even to offer consultancy services in the field of mission. As David told his story, I was all too aware that my own 'hands on' experience of evangelism was becoming further and further removed from what I was actually doing with my time. I was aware also of how often I had reasoned to myself that my 'equipping' ministry actually made me more effective in the field of evangelism than if I spent all of my time trying to do it myself. No doubt some of that rationalisation is valid—but it is also very convenient!

The staff at Willow Creek, including Bill Hybels, are personally involved in the evangelistic process, building relationships with the unchurched. The fact of their involvement is reflected in the sermon illustrations, in the teaching programme, in the conversations that are held and most of all in the degree to which the church is able to maintain the cutting edge of understanding the mind of unchurched Harry and Mary.

The practical experience of building relationships with the unchurched enables leaders to share a host of practical illustrations to inspire creative approaches to building those relationships. Despite the variety of illustrations, four categories of approach can be identified.

1. Developing the familiar

It is possible to have effective evangelistic opportunities in addition to those few special relationships that might last for a lifetime. Simply knowing people on a recognition basis will sometimes be enough to offer an invitation to an evangelistic event. Developing those kinds of relationships does not take a large investment of extra time, since many of the people that we can come to know in this way are those to whom we would normally speak; for example the people to whom we speak at the supermarket checkout, the person who operates the lift at work or the receptionist at the doctor's surgery. The point about these relationships is that we only need to make a decision to develop existing points of contact, rather than see every human contact as merely a transaction to be completed as quickly as possible.

Such a strategy will mean making some strategic decisions. For example, we might choose to make some purchases at local shops in order to get to know the local shopkeepers or their assistants on a first-name basis. As Bill Hybels points out in a talk entitled 'Rubbing Shoulders With Irreligious People', the same process can also work the other way round. The salesperson in the food shop who becomes a Christian also has many regular contacts with those who shop there which can become opportunities to build recognition relationships.

2. Common interest relationships

The past ten years have seen a huge increase in leisure activities. The United States is reputed to have more than 3,000 special-interest magazine titles, many of which are intended to meet the needs of specialist leisure activities; Europe is not far behind. All too often, Christians have not participated in activities outside the church either because the church has kept them too busy with internal church matters or because even leisure interests have been conducted entirely within Christian circles. Willow Creek actively encourages its members to have areas of service or activity outside of the church so that every member is able to maintain contact with the unchurched.

3. Community relationships

An intentional decision to be involved in community organisations such as school boards, local politics and community associations will produce a host of relationships with those whom we would never meet if we simply waited for them to come to church. Just as important as the opportunity to build relationships with others will be the effect of developing a Christian witness in society itself. All too often the very people who are sufficiently capable, and whom we need to release for this kind of activity, are those we normally rely on to run a large number of programmes within the church. Clearly, some difficult decisions with regard to priorities need to be made in this area.

4. Re-established relationships

Even though a church such as Willow Creek might urge its members to remain in contact with unchurched friends, the very process of becoming a Christian can often mean that we have unintentionally lost contact with some friends before we have ever realised that our former friendships are becoming distant.

In a sermon preached to a New Community worship service, Lee Strobel describes how he made some intentional decisions to recontact some old acquaintances.[2] He had in mind those people whom he had once spent time with in the context of his job as a journalist but with whom he had lost contact. One of those he met again was a well-known newscaster on one of the local Chicago TV stations. The news that Lee was now working for a church evidently came as something of a surprise to his former friend. But it was a point of interest and as such the opportunity for a conversation with someone who otherwise might not have had a relationship with a colleague whom he respected and who was also a Christian.

GIVING A VERBAL WITNESS

In Chapter 3, we noted the distinction that many specialists in evangelism make between being a witness and being an evangelist. While Willow Creek does recognise that such a distinction can be made, they emphasise that those who are giving a verbal witness are involved in the task of evangelism. It is not as if witnessing is one department and evangelism another. We may not all be evangelists, but all Christians are called to be a part of the evangelistic outreach of the church, just as while some are given a specific gift of mercy, all Christians are called to be merciful. Such an approach helps to avoid a situation where those who do not feel that they have the specific gift of evangelism drop out of any involvement in the evangelistic task of the church.

While it may not be possible to train people in how to build an authentic relationship, it is certainly possible to train people to give a verbal witness. Willow Creek gives a high priority to training their members in this area of evangelism. Training is given through a seminar programme which they call the Impact Evangelism Seminar. The seminar is taught every other month throughout the year, alternating each month between Sunday, Monday or Tuesday nights, with an average of 150 people attending each session. There are four two-hour sessions. Everyone in the church is encouraged to attend, and those who are committed to a small group will usually attend this event as part of their small group programme together with the other members of their group. To give some idea of the number of people trained by this means, over 2,500 people have attended between the Seminar's inception in 1988 and March 1992.

The training is intended to equip people in a number of areas. Here are a few:

1. Recognising opportunities for a verbal witness. Many Christians report that when they have been successful in building a relationship with someone, the very fact of building that relationship sometimes makes it very awkward to speak about spiritual matters. The question therefore arises, how does one turn the conversation to allow a discussion of the Christian faith so that the subject doesn't sound forced or unnatural?

Often Christians need some illustrations to help them to begin thinking about the specific opportunities afforded by their situation. One man who was in sales commented that he just didn't know how to introduce the subject of his faith with his colleagues at work. He was asked the question, 'Well, what do your colleagues normally say to you when they meet you?' He replied, 'They usually ask "How is everything going".' The suggestion that came from Willow Creek was this. 'Try responding, "As far as work is concerned, OK. Family life, great. Spiritually, fantastic. Which one do you want to talk about?" '3

2. Telling your story. Every Christian has a story but often needs help in telling it. The simple story of how a person has become a Christian and what Jesus means now is the most compelling witness that an individual can give. Bible Society in England and Wales trains Christians in how to share their story through a video programme known as Person to Person. In less than five years almost 100,000 individuals have gone through this training programme. The results have been very revealing at a number of levels.

First, the experience of both Bible Society and Willow Creek is to discover that not everyone who comes for training has a story, simply because no one has ever explained the Christian message to them! A number of people become Christians for the first time as the result of a training programme like this.

Second, it is surprising how those who have been Christians for a long time but have never talked to anyone else about their faith are liberated to be able to do so as a result of this simple training exercise. Reports of elderly people winning others to Christ for the first time in their life have been one of the features of Bible Society's experience with the Person to Person programme.

3. Leading others to a commitment to Christ. My own experience of training others in evangelism tells me that many are prepared to believe that they will have some opportunities to talk to people about their faith, but few believe that there will be many occasions when they will be asked to lead someone to a specific commitment to Christ. However, experience suggests that the unexpected keeps happening and we need to be prepared for those occasions when such a specific question arises.

Christians need to be able to do two things. First, they need to be able to give a brief presentation of the heart of the Christian message. The best-known presentation of the gospel message among evangelical Christians would either be the 'four spiritual laws' or a variation of it. Many evangelical Christians will be able to remember the diagram that depicts the chasm of sin separating man from God and the way in which the cross of Christ acts as a bridge across that chasm. It does not have to be that particular formulation that is used, but it is important to be able lucidly and simply to explain the basic ingredients of the gospel message. In fact, Willow Creek does teach the 'bridge illustration' although they do not use the precise 'four spiritual laws' presentation.

The second requirement for a Christian involved in evangelism is to be able to answer the basic question of an enquirer, 'What do I have to do in order to become a Christian?' The ability to explain to someone their need to confess their sin, to make a commitment to follow Christ and to be introduced to the importance of working that commitment out in the body of Christ is vital.

4. Offer an invitation to a Seeker Service or some other evangelistic event. The value of being able to invite someone with confidence to an evangelistic event becomes increasingly clear once one is actively involved in reaching out to others. Not only does the availability of such regular events aid the process of discussion and relationship-building, there is also the security of knowing that even if some of the attempts we make to explain the Christian message don't work out, an invitation to an event that will explain the message more fully is always there to assist us in our efforts!

The Impact Evangelism Seminars attempt to give sufficient training to allow Christians to feel competent in each of the above areas. In addition, the seminars give some other valuable advice which we can summarise as follows:

1. Be Yourself. Most evangelistic methods have the drawback of tending to force those who use it into a particular mould, which might not fit their particular personality. Willow Creek attempts to use a variety of evangelistic models which seek to demonstrate that it is possible to find an approach to evangelism that fits the personality that God has given each one of us. Not every evangelist needs to be an extrovert. Indeed, it is almost certainly the case that the group of people that we naturally mix with do so because of the personality that we already have. If we are naturally more introverted, it is almost certainly the case that we can be more effective as an evangelist if we relate to people on that basis.

2. Be specific. Rather than attempting to reach everyone that we come into contact with, it can often be more effective to list three people who are in our sphere of influence whom we can pray for and talk to regularly. Willow Creek recommends that each believer keep just three people in mind at any one time. They further suggest that should any one of those people either become a Christian or move outside that believer's sphere of influence, that they then replace them on the list with another person.

3. Use the language of our culture. Christians very quickly develop an 'in house' language which is only really understood by those who are already Christians. A conscious effort is required to explain the truths of the Christian faith in everyday language. The Impact Evangelism course uses a video enactment of someone using 'in house' language and an inappropriate approach, to overstate the point that it takes practice to constantly present the Christian faith in words which those outside of the Christian community can understand.

4. Be Prepared. The experience of Willow Creek in evangelism has enabled them to develop a range of gospel illustrations that use everyday language to explain the Christian message. Believers are encouraged to learn these basic illustrations and then to consider which ones would work best for the personality of each participant and the particular circle of friends that each person has.

5. *Know the questions.* The secular culture within which we live has a number of key objections to the claims of the Christian faith. The Impact Evangelism course highlights the most common of those objections and seeks to train Christians in how to respond to the questions that are frequently raised.

RESOURCES FOR EVANGELISM

For Willow Creek, evangelism is not so much a programme as a way of life. A concern for evangelism is built into the culture of the church. Inevitably, when such a culture prevails, the evangelistic programme tends to be undergirded by a host of other resources, each of which serves to underpin and further encourage the development of an evangelistic mindset in the church.

We have already noted that one of the strengths of the preaching at the Seeker Service is that of the applicability of the sermon to the concerns of those unchurched people who attend. As we have noted in an earlier chapter, this approach answers the unspoken question of the unbeliever who is asking, 'Does it work?' However, those who continue to seek eventually move to consider a question which is much more critical for the Christian community, namely, 'Is it true?'

The life of Willow Creek strongly features a number of activities which offer further evangelistic resources to answer this second key question. The major resources in this category can be listed as follows:

1. Bill Hybels has preached a series of sermons entitled, 'Christianity 101'. These sermons contain a presentation of the reasonableness of the Christian faith. Willow Creek regards these as such an important part of the programme that tapes of these messages are sold at less than cost price.

2. Literature on the reasons for belief is made available both to believers and to visitors. The church has a well-stocked bookshop and resource centre where such inexpensive literature can be purchased.

3. Occasional seminars are held on Sunday evening which target particularly difficult issues. These are presented in very creative ways. For example, one Sunday evening a debate on the Reality of the Resurrection was featured and heavily advertised just before Easter. Over 5,000 people attended this event.

4. Foundation classes are sometimes held before the mid-week New Community Services. These often use a series format and again target difficult issues, such as the reliability of the Bible.

5. Occasional evangelistic events other than services are arranged. These might take the form of a men's breakfast or even a golf clinic, when someone who is a professional golfer and also a Christian can combine a practical demonstration of their ability with a testimony of the relevance of their Christian faith.

6. A team known as the 'In Touch' team is trained to respond to the fifty or so requests that come in each week for more information on the church. These requests come from a tear-off slip that is provided as part of the weekly Seeker Service programme. The form has a number of options which allow the respondent to indicate the kind of information that he or she is seeking. Willow Creek is very careful to offer only the information that is specifically requested and does not seek to prematurely evangelise the enquirer. The church attempts to follow up every weekend inquiry by the Tuesday evening following the service at which the form is handed in. The team is trained, however, to look for God's open doors among those who enquire in this way and to seize evangelistic opportunities that are ripe.

7. Another team has been developed consisting of those who enjoy the intellectual challenge of apologetics. This group is known as 'The Defenders'. They regularly receive training in issues such as how to respond creatively to the claims of various cults, other religions and more recently, the New Age movement. This group acts as a resource to others in the church who have been confronted with difficult questions in the course of their evangelistic endeavours.

THE FRONTLINE TEAM

The clear emphasis of Willow Creek is to mobilise as many people as possible in the church in the evangelistic task. However, the church recognises that there are individuals who are particularly gifted in the area of evangelism. For them, evangelism is a passion. There is always a temptation to take such people and form them into a team in a manner that actually harms the evangelistic ministry. The separation of evangelists from the rest of the church not only prevents the other ministries of a church from receiving their creative contribution as evangelists but also produces a culture where those who do not feel that they have an evangelistic gift can assume that the task of evangelism has been delegated to those who are gifted and separated out into the evangelistic team.

The policy of Willow Creek has therefore been to allow those with evangelistic gifts to be involved in all the other ministries of the church, believing that this will assist each activity to keep an evangelistic cutting edge. However, the disadvantage of this policy has been to produce a situation where those with an evangelistic gift and call tend to feel undersupported and sometimes isolated. The response of Willow Creek has been to create the 'Frontline Team'. This group was formed in March 1991 but the meetings were scheduled sufficiently infrequently for no one to feel under such pressure that they needed to drop out of their existing involvement in the church. The approach of those leading the Frontline Team has been to encourage the team members to see their current ministry involvement as the place where they can be increasingly effective as evangelists.

What then does the team do together? There are currently almost 300 people who would identify themselves with the Frontline Team with something like 200 active and regular participants. Their practical involvement with the team consists of attending bi-monthly meetings on a Saturday morning and communicating to the ministry's leaders, Lee Strobel and Mark Mittelburg, the names of those people who have been led to Christ by team members.

The Saturday morning sessions are varied but each is

designed to give practical help and encouragement to those who attend. Typically, a team meeting would begin with breakfast and would finish by 11.00 am. Generally 150 - 200 team members attend. The content of these meetings includes some specific teaching on evangelism and the sharing of factual accounts by the team members telling how they have led particular individuals to Christ. Occasionally the team will have a celebration to give thanks for the fruitfulness of the ministry of those in the team. A recent celebration held in December 1991 featured seven people who had made a commitment to Christ through the activities of the team members. Each told the story of their conversion from the perspective of one who was being evangelised.

Occasionally, the group sponsors its own special evangelistic events to which the team members invite their contacts. Usually these events are low-key, socially orientated, occasions designed to encourage sufficient interest for people to return to visit the more hard-hitting weekend services. One example is an event at which a well-known sports broadcaster was invited to speak about his profession and the part that his Christian commitment plays in his life and work.

Frontline Team members are also given advance notification of any upcoming events that would offer good opportunities to invite contacts, such as special services, new preaching series, or any events organised by other groups in the church. Lee Strobel, who keeps the statistics of those who have made a commitment through the activities of this team, has identified 170 people who became Christians in the period March–December 1991. This figure emphasises that whereas Willow Creek generally is concerned with the evangelistic process, the Frontline Team is strongly focused on the evangelistic result.

The Frontline Team is still in the early stages of its development and it may be that there will come a need to change and adapt some of the activities in which it engages. So too with many of the other evangelistic initiatives of Willow Creek. The diversity of their activity is a sign of dynamic life and of an evangelistic heart. As a church, Willow Creek would agree with the words of Michael Green:

> Evangelism is not an optional extra for those who like that sort of thing. It is a major part of the obedience of the whole church to the command of its Lord. He told us to go out into all the world and make disciples. It is hard to see how we can realistically acknowledge him as Lord if we take no notice of what he tells us to do.[4]

FOOTNOTES

1. Otniel Bunaciu, *Congregational Quarterly*, vol 9 no 4 (1991): p 5.

2. The sermon referred to is entitled 'Eternal Turning Points'.

3. This illustration can be found in the talk by Bill Hybels, 'Rubbing Shoulders with Irreligious People'.

4. Michael Green, *Evangelism Through the Local Church* (Hodder and Stoughton: 1990), p 6.

CHAPTER SEVEN

Building a New Community

WRITING ABOUT THE PLACE of the local church in evangelism, Michael Green comments:

> Mission is one half of the reason for the church's existence; worship is the other. In these two ways we are called to display what it means to be a 'colony of heaven'.[1]

Other thinkers in the field of evangelism also testify to the vital place of worship in relation to the life of the church. William Abraham writing on the theory and practice of evangelism says:

> To make evangelism the primary concern of the church is to give it a misplaced and exaggerated position in our lives. The first task of the church is to worship: to bow down before the Lord of glory, to celebrate God's love and majesty, and to invite God to rule over the length and breadth of all creation.[2]

This healthy concern to see worship as a vital centre of concern for a church which is strongly evangelistic in orientation actually says something about the very purpose for which the church exists and towards which its evangelistic efforts are directed. To quote Lesslie Newbigin:

> Jesus, as I said earlier, did not write a book but formed a community. This community has at its heart the remembering and rehearsing of his words and deeds, and the sacraments given by him through which it is enabled both to engraft new members into its life and to renew this life again and again through sharing in his risen life through the body broken and the lifeblood poured out. It exists in him and for him. He is the centre of its life. Its character is given to it, when it is true to its nature, not by the characters of its members but by his character. Insofar as it is true to its calling, it becomes the place where men and women and children find that the gospel gives them the framework of understanding, the 'lenses' through which they are able to understand and cope with the world.[3]

Evangelism has no purpose unless it is directed to the building of a community which seeks to reflect the character of Jesus. Without a commitment to such a community, evangelism is reduced to mere recruitment and the truth of the gospel message becomes only a form of religious indoctrination. But if too much effort is directed towards evangelism, will there be sufficient energy left over for the creating of such a community? William Abraham points out that a church should ensure that the worshipping community be given a high priority, not only for the sake of a right balance in the church itself but even in order to preserve the evangelistic zeal of the church. Abraham notes:

> Evangelism is hard work; it is difficult to keep Christians motivated in this area; it repeatedly falls into disfavor so that prophets have to arise and call the church back to the task. It is only reasonable, therefore, that in frustration and eagerness some should seek to foster its significance by insisting that it be absolutely primary. In the long run, however, the consequences of this course will catch up with

us. It will lead to an unhealthy situation where worship will be utilitarian, where converts will be anemic and unbalanced, and where sheep will look up and not be fed.[4]

Ironically, therefore, the only proper safeguard for evangelism is for us to see it in its proper place as something which is balanced with the task of building the community of the believers itself.

WORSHIP IN THE NEW COMMUNITY

A vital insight of Willow Creek has been to recognise that the needs of the unchurched and the needs of believers are very different. We have discussed in some detail the practical application of this insight in terms of the creation of a Seeker Service. The creativity of Willow Creek in relation to the Seeker Service concept, a church for the unchurched, is arguably the aspect of Willow Creek's life that has caused it to become well known. However, what is not so well known is the commitment of Willow Creek to invest just as much effort in meeting the needs of the believers as they do in attempting to create a Seeker Service for the unchurched.

Those who attend the Seeker Service and are already Christians will quickly realise that worship, in the sense in which believers understand worship, has not really occurred. The uninformed believer who draws the hasty conclusion that the Seeker Service is all that defines Willow Creek will quickly move to another church to have his or her needs met. In the same way, those who come as seekers but find that their questions are being answered will also begin to find the need for something more than the regular explanation of basic Christian principles, no matter how attractively presented, which forms the heart of the Seeker Service on a Sunday. It is essential for such a person to also attend one of the mid-week, New Community Services, held on Wednesday and Thursday evenings.

Willow Creek has demonstrated not only that they understand the needs of unchurched Harry and Mary very well indeed, but they also appreciate the essential heartbeat and concerns of the person that they call 'believing Bob'. Most important of all they understand that most of their 'believing Bobs' will come to the New Community worship service feeling very stressed and worn out. More than that, many who attend will feel that in some way or another they have compromised their faith or failed the God whom they worship. In short, the leaders of Willow Creek understand that one of the requirements of worship for the believers at their church will be to encourage, refresh and inspire people who will not have arrived at the service brimming over with faith and enthusiasm. Secondly, they know from long experience that because the worship service for believers is during the week and not on Sundays, that they will always have to work hard to encourage people to attend the New Community worship service. For both these reasons, it is essential that there be the same commitment to quality at the New Community Service that is evident at the Seeker Service.

When Willow Creek does succeed in persuading people to attend mid-week and when the New Community Service does inspire those who attend, the event makes a very important contribution to the quality of the Christian life and witness of the members of the church. Some 5,000 to 6,000 people attend the New Community Services each week. The provision of this mid-week event is not just important for meeting needs that are not met on a Sunday. Many Christians, even those who do have a more traditional worship service on a Sunday, experience to some degree a mid-week sense of failure and stress. The New Community services also help to address this need.

As with many other aspects of the programme at Willow Creek, there has been a difficult learning curve in developing a deep sense of worship at the New Community Services. At the church leaders' conferences, Nancy Beach tells of how in the early days of the church what passed for worship at the mid-week believers meeting was hardly worship at all. She describes what took place then as a strong teaching sermon with a song-time added on. At best, in the early days of their life as a church, they could have been described as a church where individuals knew how to worship God on their own, but where there was little corporate adoration of God.

As Willow Creek began to look at what other churches did in their worship services, they began to realise that they had not really understood the nature of worship. With their original format, the event was really only as inspiring as the teaching time could make it. While a good teaching sermon would often encourage those with a very cerebral approach, it didn't minister to the whole person.

Bill Hybels acknowledges his debt to other churches, particularly charismatic churches, who taught him that the heart of worship involves leading believers into a direct and personal experience of God; not just as individuals, but as a corporate body. As Bill Hybels brought these insights back to Willow Creek, they found that it was necessary almost to refound the New Community Service. This was accomplished by a combination of teaching on the true nature of worship and the giving of such a strong lead from the platform that they were able to model for the believers present something of what it means to worship God as a body of believers. Bill Hybels has sufficient musical gifts to be able to teach and lead the worship for long enough for the worship culture of the church to become completely recast.

The experience of Willow Creek has been that the discovery of corporate worship at a deeper level than that which they had previously known has become a vital component in terms of equipping and enabling the church members. This assists their response to the visionary challenges that are constantly put before them. Knowing what needs to be done is not enough. It is also necessary for a Christian's experience of God to be rich enough for him or her to want to share something of that experience with those they meet. Worship at the New Community Service has become the replenishing well of living water, without which the evangelistic zeal of Willow Creek would almost certainly dry up.

What then are the particular insights that the church tries to include in the New Community Service to help keep the worship alive? First, and most important, the worship leader is chosen with great care. The person who leads is not acting as an announcer simply to take the congregation through a set programme of items. Specific gifts are needed in order to lead a worship event in such a way that it will be truly worshipful. As we have suggested above, worship is something that involves encouraging people to respond at a *feeling* level. People need to feel secure in their worship environment before they can respond at such a level. Only some people have the gift of leading worship in such a way that the congregation will be able to respond at the feeling level.

Secondly, the worship leader has the key responsibility for selecting the songs and basic worship theme for the evening. While some help is available from the music team or from other team members who will be sharing in the service, the ultimate responsibility for choosing the songs remains with the worship leader. It is essential for worship leaders to prepare themselves in prayer as they come to choose the theme and songs for the service. Once the theme and songs have been chosen, then the other team members can respond with their contribution, whether that be drama or special music or any other contribution. As part of the process of choosing songs, two questions are asked. Are the words true? And is the music singable? Both ingredients are important. It is all too easy for leaders to choose songs with good tunes but with words that do not honestly reflect Christian experience. Willow Creek tries hard to maintain integrity in terms of the words of the songs that they choose. Sometimes songs that have good words have tunes which are not easy to sing on a congregational basis. Such a phenomenon applies more to newer songs, largely because older songs with weak tunes are no longer sung. Willow Creek tries to maintain a good mix of new material and quality older hymns.

Thirdly and perhaps surprisingly, in view of the programme approach that is taken to the Seekers Services, Willow Creek does not necessarily attempt to present a unified theme between the worship time and the sermon. Sometimes the two will fit together well but essentially the thirty to forty minutes worship is seen as standing on its own, separate from the teaching time. This view is taken because the teaching may well be following a theme over a number of weeks and it could easily become very artificial to attempt to fit a worship experience into a teaching theme. The attempt of the worship time is much more to try to gain a sense of what the Spirit is saying to the whole church. Such a concern requires more flexibility than would be possible if the worship theme always had to be tied to the message. The priority is the worship though it may well be that the preacher will need to take account of what has happened in the worship time.

Fourthly, there is an attempt to vary the mood and content of the worship time from week to week. Willow Creek makes the valid observation that worship can easily become very predictable. Even in charismatic churches that claim not to have a fixed order of service, in many cases those who attend soon come to know what to expect. Those who love the charismatic renewal recognise that it has not discovered the final answer in terms of worship that is forever fresh and enriching. Indeed there can scarcely be anything more deadly than a predictable pentecostal or charismatic service where the same people can be relied on to give rather similar prophecies week after week!

In any case, whether charismatic in tradition or not, it is vital that worship should not become predictable. Willow Creek puts a great deal of thought and prayer into considering the direction in which the worship needs to flow. On some occasions the worship begins quietly and builds towards a sense of rejoicing. At other times it will begin with joy and gradually become more reflective. Many other variations are possible, the important ingredient is a prayerful preparation that properly understands that which is needed for the worship of the body as a whole.

DISCIPLESHIP IN THE NEW COMMUNITY

The natural progression for someone who has started to attend a Seeker Service and then has become a regular attender at the

New Community worship is to become a participant in a small group. Willow Creek is currently going through a major change in relation to its small groups. Until very recently, there was only one type of small group, namely two-year discipleship groups. More recently, the church has added two other types of small groups to its programme, which they describe as task groups and community groups.

Task groups, as the name suggests, consist of those individuals who are meeting together to fulfil a specific objective or ministry. The value of meeting together as a group in order to contribute to a ministry goal is that an element of mutually supportive fellowship is combined with the ministry.

Community groups are intended to provide shorter-term, informal groups for those people who are not yet ready to commit themselves to a discipleship group but want to become slightly more involved in the church by having a 'taster' of what a small group experience might be like. These groups also provide an opportunity to keep contact with people who have started to attend on a regular basis but who might otherwise be lost to the church because there is no easy or obvious point of contact. In this sense, Community Groups act as friendship groups within the congregation.

The leaders chosen to run these groups are selected for their ability to make friends easily and are given the task of 'fishing' for potential group members in the pool of those who have been attending for a short time. This not only fills the groups but also ensures that some people are constantly looking to build relationships in a situation that so emphasises anonymity that Willow Creek might be in danger of seeming like an unwelcoming church. Community Groups help the church to keep the balance between a lack of pressure to join anything and a feeling of being welcomed.

Important as these new types of groups are becoming in terms of the overall development of Willow Creek, in this section we will focus our attention on the nature of the longer-running discipleship groups. Willow Creek thinks of a discipleship group as consisting of 8 to 10 people who will be committed to meet weekly for a two-year programme comprising 68 sessions (although recently, a further editing of this material has produced a slightly shorter course which newly formed groups will be adopting in the future). Approximately 1,000 people are involved in the discipleship groups at any one time.

It is quite a daunting commitment, not just in terms of the length of the programme but also in terms of the content of the material itself. Those who attend are not just passive spectators but are expected to participate in developing strong relationships within the group, by revealing something of who they are and by sharing in assignments outside of the group sessions. The group sessions consist of a fairly demanding two-hour programme, a commitment which should not be entered into by the fainthearted!

The creation of such a demanding structure for their small groups is a critical part of the Willow Creek strategy. The central intention of the programme is to enable those who join the church to be properly discipled. To a very large extent, the effectiveness of the whole church rests on the degree to which the discipleship ingredient of the small group programme succeeds in its goal of encouraging members to become devoted followers of Jesus Christ.

Willow Creek points to three important ingredients for a successful small group discipleship programme; the right leader, the right match of people in the group and the right material to study.

1. The right leader. Generally leaders are 'talent spotted' through the discipleship process itself. Those who are already leading groups are asked to look for potential leaders among those that they are teaching. Sometimes group members will actually volunteer to lead a group, other times they will be invited to consider such a role.

2. The right match of people. Those who are interested in joining a small group are asked to fill out a form which invites them to list their background, interests and experience as a Christian. A staff person then attempts to match people as nearly as possible with those who have been Christians for a similar length of time and with those who are of a similar age and have common interests. The intention is to attempt to produce groups composed of people who will be able to share easily and naturally with others in the group.

After this initial attempt to 'mix and match', group members are invited to two socially orientated events during which time they can try out the group to see if they feel comfortable. There is an agreement that anyone is free to contract out at this stage and try another group.

3. *The right material.* Willow Creek has put a great deal of effort into creating the right material for their programme. As you might expect, it has not been possible for the church to find exactly what they were looking for among the material that has already been published and they have therefore written their own very comprehensive leader's guide and student worksheets. The principles which underlie the material and its use are just as important as the content of the material itself.

Three key principles are evident.

The building of relationships is key. The material is designed to promote a high degree of sharing and mutual accountability. To some extent the concern for relationships reflects the experience of Bill Hybels in his early Son City days. Speaking to a group of church leaders and clergy, Bill Hybels reflected on the strength of relationships which he encountered in a small group of four people. He said of this experience:

> When a senior pastor has had his heart knit together with some brothers and has felt what it's like to impart the Christian life to others and see people come to maturity and take up reins of leadership and disciple other people who then disciple other people, then he can talk about discipleship with a ring of authority in his voice that shakes people on a really deep level.[5]

The practice of transparent relationships is key. The relationships that are built are not just based on coming to know the other members of the group well in terms of shared interests. More importantly the small groups offer an arena in which the participants can discover an ingredient in Willow

Creek's culture which it is difficult to describe, but which we might call a radical commitment to a transparent honesty. Such a commitment can be illustrated very clearly by reference to the kinds of questions that Willow Creek might ask potential employees. For example, Don Cousins, who is responsible for personnel issues, lists some of the questions that he would be likely to ask potential employees of Willow Creek. Writing on spiritual authenticity he says:

> I ask specific questions to detect this quality, such as: 'What have you studied in your quiet times this week? Can you share some recent answers to prayer? What are the temptations you struggle with most? How did you come to know Christ? Have you been discipled? Have you discipled someone else?' These questions get at the heart of a person's walk with God more than a general, 'How's your spiritual life?'[6]

Application to actual lifestyle is important. There is a real concern to avoid only imparting information, or Bible knowledge, to people. Valuable as knowledge might be, there is a concern to see knowledge applied in such a way that it actually changes the way in which people live. In the words of the leaders' manual, 'Others will articulate the right answers but their schedules, checkbooks and neighbors tell a different story.' The leader is advised:

> Don't let their familiarity with spiritual matters blind you (or them) to ways they're not consistently living out some aspect of their Christian walk. Ask some uncomfortable questions. Get beneath the appearances.[7]

Helping people to relate directly to God is essential. The way in which the material is handled focuses people again and again on their actual relationship with God and particularly on the quality of their prayer life. Even the homework assignments are designed to be 'appointments with God'. In other words, the material suggests that the best framework in which to tackle the weekly group assignments is the daily prayer time. However well people relate to each other, they will not really be disciples unless they have also made 'a fresh discovery of the God who loves them, who has sought them out, who enjoys His relationship with them and wants them to enjoy their relationships with Him'.[8]

The materials covers four main areas:

First, *walking with God*. This foundational study deals with some areas that would be very commonly found in study programmes used by evangelical Christians. Topics such as Christian assurance, the Bible as the word of God, prayer, the work of the Holy Spirit and Christian obedience are all explored in some depth.

Second, *learning about Christ*. Again, one would expect to find many of the topics in this section in many evangelical Bible studies on the person of Christ. Themes such as the Old Testament prophecies concerning Christ, the coming of Christ, and elements of his life, teaching and person leading up to his death and resurrection are all covered in some detail.

Third, *discovering the church*. The material which is taught in this section may very well be missing from the agenda of some evangelicals. Willow Creek has a strong sense of the importance of the church in the plan and purpose of God. Dr Gilbert Bilezikian, a founding elder at Willow Creek and the man whom Bill Hybels describes as his mentor, tells of his discovery of the importance of the church in this way:

> Having become a believer apart from the church, I felt little need to become involved in the church. Participation in church life seemed to be an optional decision, somewhat desirable but not indispensable or mandated by Scripture.
>
> Some years later, I was invited to pastor a young and dynamic church in a suburb of Albany, New York. It was during this intense and all-absorbing ministry that I discovered the biblical doctrine of the church. Far from being a motley gathering of wimpy people, I discovered the church to be the new community that God was preparing on earth for an eternal destiny in heaven. The church is at the very center of everything that God is doing....

Once I had acquired this perspective of the primacy of the church, the implications became clear for the conduct of our lives as Christians, for the use of our gifts and resources... The church was to be the warm, open, pulsating, dynamic, loving, attractive new community of God's people that would penetrate culture and claim it for Christ.[9]

Something of that vision is communicated in this section of the discipleship group material. Probably the most important ingredient is a very comprehensive series on 'Making a Contribution through Service'. The heart of this material helps members to see the importance of the place of the church in the plan and purpose of God for his world.

Fourth, *impacting the world*. This section includes a four-week exposure to the Impact Evangelism Seminar which has been described in the previous chapter. The intention of this section is to finally equip, and then assist, each group member to discover an avenue of service in the church.

The discipleship process plays a critical part in preparing teams of workers who enable the ministry of Willow Creek to have the kind of cutting edge that allows the church to continue to grow, not by attracting other Christians, but by reaching out to the unchurched and then, in turn, discipling them. Bill Hybels attempts to describe something of that team effort when speaking to a church leaders' conference in the following way:

And when you really love the church, then you've got to be a part of it and you've got to die to self and live for Christ through the church. Once people hear enough of that teaching and sense in our hearts that we really feel that way, then you get that feeling of abandonment sweeping over the church, and you have people who say with great joy: 'Whatever it takes.'

It was thirty-one degrees below zero one night last winter and we had 35 lay people out directing traffic in our parking lot before and after a service. They didn't get a dime for doing it. They huddled together and held hands and thanked God for the privilege of serving in His church. That's whatever it takes.[10]

LIFESTYLE IN THE NEW COMMUNITY

As you might expect, Willow Creek teaches the principle of tithing. However, their view of giving is much more comprehensive than a concern for the weekly offering. Their approach is to place giving in the context of lifestyle, a concern which is summed up by the word 'stewardship'.

Teaching on money starts with the assumption that some who join the church from a secular background will not be able to tithe. There is a recognition that the values of an acquisitive society impact many people in such a way that people can very often be spending up to and beyond their normal level of income. Thus, those who join Willow Creek will very likely need help in learning a new set of values in order to even begin a regular practice of tithing. Such a process takes time. Willow Creek teaches its members not to live on credit, but instead to value saving as a means of purchasing goods, to pay cash instead of accumulating debts, or in other words to live within one's means.

Nor is this just a matter of changing the method of payment. It is a matter of changing expectations about what it is normal for someone to possess. Bill Hybels and the other staff members attempt to model that change of expectations in their own life style. In the case of Bill Hybels, the car he drives is a standard model and is several years old. He has asked for his own salary to be frozen at the level at which he was paid in 1985.

A celebrated sermon topic for the New Community Service has been 'The Story of Seven Demotions', based on Philippians 2:5–11. The point of the sermon is to emphasise that Jesus offered a model of sacrifice and downgrading of his own status in order to please God. The sermon is used to point out that the concern of our current culture for constant upward mobility runs directly counter to the values modelled by Jesus. One could be forgiven for assuming that such a message would not often be preached in those American churches which target the babyboomers occupying employment positions of middle management and above, but at Willow Creek, it is!

The effect of this encouragement to reassess lifestyle is to allow the release of funds not just for the maintenance of the internal life of the church and its outreach programme, but also for the establishment of a significant benevolence programme. The basic philosophy of this programme is contained in the following four statements:

1. Needy people matter to God.

2. No member of the body of Christ should be without food, shelter and basic transportation needs.

3. God's people are commanded to care for each other.

4. Although money is a need, meeting that need is usually not a final solution to an individual's practical problems in general.

This basic philosophy is applied in the first instance to those who are members or attenders of Willow Creek, but the church also exercises benevolence towards those who are in need beyond the immediate boundaries of the church. When people who are not church members or attenders are referred to the church for help, Willow Creek utilises a social service programme which assesses the need and the degree to which the person wishes to take some responsibility for their own future. The church tries to give priority to those who will work with the church for change in key areas of their life. For example, if a person's practical need has come about because of addiction to alcohol or drugs, then the church offers a recovery programme. It is unlikely that Willow Creek will continue to help those who do not wish to take advantage of any of the referral services that are available.

As the philosophy suggests, although money is given the benevolence ministry also has a range of other practical resources at its disposal. These include a budget counselling service, a job-search support scheme, a food support project and the facility to offer a range of free professional services such as legal, medical, dental and tax advice.

In addition to these services, the church has recently begun a project which utilises the skills of motor mechanics in the church. Although it may sound strange to European ears, cars are not luxuries in the United States. It is difficult to shop, socialise or even maintain employment without a vehicle in suburban North America. Church members are encouraged to give their old cars to the church and the motor mechanics ensure that they are in good order before giving them away to people in need. The same team undertakes to repair at no cost the vehicles of those people who are in need and who cannot afford to have their cars repaired.

The extent of the benevolence programme is considerable. During 1991, 50 cars were repaired and given away; a further 85 were repaired. 2,060 man hours were expended in this way. 78,340 units of food were collected and given away. The net worth of these gifts amounted to $100,283. The total amount of food that was provided was the equivalent to one week of food for 3,668 people.

The statistics are impressive both in terms of finance and time expended. But more important than the quantity of help offered is the fundamental principle that makes it possible for the church to release such resources. The principle of a moderate lifestyle that seeks to challenge the prevailing cultural norm which always proclaims that more is better, is foundational in terms of the kind of church that Willow Creek seeks to be.

Clearly, Willow Creek is hardly unique in terms of its emphasis on the creation of stewardship and a strong community life. Nevertheless it is valid to recognise that Willow Creek does have a strong commitment to create disciples and not just converts. So much attention has been focused on the Seekers Service concept that the concern of Willow Creek to create disciples might easily be missed. Yet it would be impossible for Willow Creek to maintain its programme of outreach and evangelism if discipleship was not at the centre of its life.

In a very real sense, the effectiveness of Willow Creek in producing disciples is in many ways more critical than the precise strategy that has been chosen to reach others. It is the discipleship programme that allows the large-scale mobilisation of people resources which has featured so strongly in the life of Willow Creek. No matter how impressive a Seeker Service presentation might be, a church with no disciples in it would see little lasting fruit from that or any other evangelistic programme. Only disciples can be properly mobilised in the service of God.

FOOTNOTES

1. Michael Green, *Evangelism Through the Local Church* (Hodder and Stoughton: 1990), p 9.

2. William Abraham, *The Logic of Evangelism* (Hodder and Stoughton: 1989), p 182.

3. Lesslie Newbigin, *The Gospel in a Pluralist Society* (SPCK: 1989), p 227.

4. William Abraham, *The Logic of Evangelism* (Hodder and Stoughton: 1989), p 182.

5. Bill Hybels, Transcript of a seminar entitled, 'Transferable Concepts from WCCC', p 12.

6. Don Cousins, *Mastering Church Management* (Multnomah Press: 1990), p 120.

7. Small Group Study Curriculum, Leader Guide, p 14.

8. *Ibid.*

9. 'Into The Stratosphere', *Willow Creek Magazine*, vol 2 no 2 (Nov/Dec 1990): p 21.

10. Bill Hybels, Transcript of a seminar entitled, 'Transferable Concepts from WCCC', p 16f.

CHAPTER EIGHT

Liberating the Gift of Leadership

THOSE WHO ARE IN the ministry sometimes refer light-heartedly to the '80-20' rule which indicates that in many churches 80% of the work is done by 20% of the people. This guideline, in many cases, applies to finance just as much as to person-hours. Some years ago the father of the Church Growth movement, Donald McGavran, carried out research to discover what relationship such a tendency had to the growth of the church. He found that those churches which succeeded in mobilising 50% or more of their membership were almost always growing churches.[1]

Reassuring though the results of such research may be, most Christian leaders know from their own experience that the mobilisation of church members represents a critical factor in the growth of any church. Indeed, Church Growth research from around the world demonstrates that although some growth factors are culturally determined and are therefore more important in some cultures than others, the growth factor of a mobilised membership transcends all cultures. It is not only a biblical principle that ministry belongs to the whole body of Christ, it is also part of the way in which God has designed human communities that participation on the basis of

God-given gifts and abilities carries with it the potential for creative power.

However, it is one thing to know that this is so and quite another to actually mobilise the Christian communities of which we are a part. It is no coincidence that nominalism is one of the most frequently cited causes of decline amongst churches. Very few experts on Church Growth are able to offer easy solutions to those church leaders who cry out that their church is in a state of severe stagnation due to the nominal commitment of their membership. Nominalism produces a creeping death. It stifles worship, it stunts giving and thwarts the offering of members' gifts and abilities.

The level of participation in Willow Creek was very high even before the launch of the church. The group that came from the Son City days did not come with the intention of simply occupying seats. Nearly all of the 125 or so young people were idealistic activists who were fired by a vision and had already been used to working hard as part of a team. It is not at all surprising that a group of young people who had already seen unusual and encouraging results in an earlier project would be prepared to maintain a high level of involvement in the new project. What has been more surprising is the continuance of a high degree of mobilisation among what is now a largely adult congregation. How has it been possible for Willow Creek to maintain such a significant level of activity?

Willow Creek points to their view of the gift of leadership as a critical factor in their ability to constantly motivate and involve large numbers of people in the ministry of the church. They would claim that the quality of leadership in a church is likely to be more important as an issue than such questions as the precise details of the programme, the worship services and the building.

WHAT DO WE MEAN BY LEADERSHIP?

In a wide-ranging survey of the importance of leadership in church planting, Stuart Christine points to the conclusion reached by studies from around the world. The adequacy of the leadership is again and again cited as critical for the success or failure of church planting.[2] It is not just a question of having leaders, but of having leaders who are sufficiently gifted to do the job that the church is asking them to do.

Hopefully, in most cases churches appoint people to leadership positions because they have leadership gifts. Surprisingly, that is not always the case. But whenever those who do not have leadership gifts are appointed to leadership positions, they never become leaders simply by occupying the post.

Bill Hybels cites Romans 12:6–8 to indicate the importance of the spiritual gift of leadership. 'We have different gifts, according to the grace given us...if it is leadership, let him govern diligently.' However, it is one thing to point to a single scripture which refers to the gift of leadership. It is quite another to arrive at an adequate biblical view of leadership.

Perhaps surprisingly, in view of its importance to the church, there are very few scriptures which refer to the specific gift or charism of leadership, although there are many scriptures that tell the story of those who clearly were leaders. This paucity of scriptures on leadership helps to explain why Christians have so much difficulty in arriving at a clear definition of what a leader is. Nor are Christians alone in finding such definition difficult. John Finney, in his book on leadership, points to the wide range of available definitions both in the Christian and the secular world.[3]

As Finney comments, some definitions 'tend to emphasise the element of "control" whereby one person influences the actions of another in a desired direction'.[4] Clearly, the leader who cannot persuade others to follow them would be rather ineffective, but the question of the degree to which 'control' as compared with the 'enabling' of others is the goal of leadership is a matter of some contention.

Just as contentious is the question of whether leaders are 'born' or 'made'. Some argue strongly that leadership is part of an innate giftedness which a person is simply born with. The very phrase 'a born leader' is part of our vocabulary. Others point to the fact that it requires a unique combination of circumstances, experiences and opportunities in order for any natural leadership gifts to be released. Eddie Gibbs produces something of a balance between these views when he says, 'Effective leadership depends on the right person being in the right place at the right time.'[5]

Whatever view one takes of the precise balance of these issues, Willow Creek is convinced that the gift of leadership is much more widespread than the church has often supposed. More importantly, it is possible to create an environment which will stimulate men and women to offer their leadership gift in the service of the Kingdom. In other words, it is possible for the church to creatively act so that it is much more likely that the right person will be found for the right situation at the right time.

FINDING A POINT PERSON

As we have indicated in an earlier chapter, Don Cousins leads a very frank session entitled 'The Hard Knocks of the Early Years' as a regular part of the leaders' conferences held at Willow Creek. Foremost among those early hard lessons came the realisation that running programmes on the basis of need alone just did not work. Experience taught them that if they began a programme in response to a need but without a key leader who was both gifted and motivated to develop the programme, before long the programme would end up becoming the responsibility of those who were already overloaded with other commitments. Usually, that meant the staff member who made the original appointment.

Their solution was to refuse to run any programme without a key leader or 'point person' who would point the way in terms of leading the programme. Such a refusal can be costly. Don Cousins describes the implications of this strategy for one area of the church's life:

When Willow Creek faced the need for a junior high ministry, we decided to take a different approach. We made the difficult decision to put the need on hold until we found a qualified leader who could make that ministry his or her speciality.

We went four years without a junior high ministry—no youth meetings, no Sunday school, nothing. Parents asked us what we were doing for junior high kids, and we had to gulp and say, 'We're looking for a leader, but right now we can't meet your needs.'

We took a lot of heat from parents when there was nothing for their kids, but we knew a first-rate ministry would require a specialized leader. Only if we had the right person, with the right gifts, doing what he or she did best—and only then—could we expect great results.[6]

Later, in the same passage, Don Cousins goes on to explain how they did find the right person for their junior high ministry, and he describes something of the subsequent success of that ministry. He closes his illustration with the following daunting sentence. 'It's a lot harder to undo and redo a weak program than to build a quality program from scratch.'

The same thinking was in evidence when Willow Creek refused to operate a missions programme for many years. It is almost unthinkable for a North American evangelical church not to have a missions programme, but Willow Creek did not have one until they found the right 'point person' to lead it. Once again, their refusal to act without a leader was a costly decision. Their inaction was sometimes misinterpreted as being an anti-missions stance. A few members of the congregation who were committed to missions did not feel able to stay in a church which had no visible missions programme. Today, the church does have a highly visible and significant missions programme, but only because they found the right leader.

In a sermon on the gift of leadership, Bill Hybels describes three abilities that a good leader or 'point person' must have if they are going to be able to lead any programme effectively. First, he says that *a good leader must be able to 'develop and cast' a vision*. This requires more than just the ability to reflect, analyse and communicate. Much more vital is that the key leader has a passion and a commitment to the vision that he or she has formulated. A leader desires to see their vision come into being so much that they are willing to make sacrifices of time, money and energy to see it come into being.

Don Cousins, describing the man they eventually found to build their junior high ministry, says, 'Eventually he developed such a zeal for that age group that he quit his job and joined our staff.' The ingredient of passion was critical to the level of commitment which he clearly displayed to that area of ministry. That same quality is reflected in the life of another individual described by Don Cousins:

> The man who runs our small-group ministry owned a real estate company before he joined our staff. A year or so before he came on staff, he said to me, 'I can tell my passion is changing. I used to want to pour all my time into the marketplace. Now I've tasted what it is to be used by God, and I want to invest myself more fully in things that really matter.'[7]

His perception of what it was that really mattered was clearly critical in terms of allowing him to be effective as a 'point person'. His passion helped him to identify what it was that he wanted to see happen and then to seek ways of communicating that passion to others.

Bill Hybels points to a second necessary ability. *A good leader will be able to draw together a team that will help him to accomplish his vision.* That process involves the ability to recognise the gifts of others and then to work with those people in such a way that they become functioning team members, each one being placed in a position where they are able to give of their best.

In many ways this is the most difficult task of all. We are all familiar with the cry of the harassed pastor, 'Church would be great if it wasn't for the people!' People can be difficult to work with. They have needs as well as gifts. They can let you down, change their commitment to something else or simply make mistakes. You can also make mistakes in choosing the wrong people or in failing to place a person in exactly the right position. But imperfect as it may be as a means of getting the task done, there is no alternative for a leader but to work with people.

The third ability is that *a good leader should be able to manage change*. Not only do organisations not stand still, but as Don Cousins points out, 'Growth inevitably leads to chaos.' [8] The same writer goes on to comment:

> Unfortunately, some leaders believe their primary responsibility is to keep the ministry running smoothly, to check chaos at any cost. So they devote the bulk of their time to the immediate tasks that keep their ministry under control. They maintain the ministry. They put out fires. But they never take the steps that would move their ministry forward. [9]

The ability to recognise that a change is needed, and to risk the short-term chaos that may well result as a consequence of both introducing and managing that change, is an essential ability in a good leader.

But abilities and qualities are not quite the same thing. As well as looking for those gifted individuals who have the right *abilities* which mark them out as potential leaders, it is also vital to select people with certain good leadership *qualities*.

THE QUALITIES OF A GOOD LEADER

Don Cousins has written very persuasively on this subject. He begins with the sobering comment:

> In seeking leaders, the temptation is to look first for an individual with tremendous gifts and abilities. At Willow Creek, however, we've learned that's not the place to start. [10]

He goes on to identify four key areas which are critically important in looking at the personal qualities of a potential leader. The first and most important area is that of *character*.

We've learned we can't compromise character. No matter how gifted, trained, or spiritually mature a person is, the true usefulness of those attributes will be determined by character.[11]

The second area is that of *spiritual authenticity*. Willow Creek is aware that it is impossible for someone to function well in the area of leadership if their own lives do not authentically reflect the same spiritual reality into which they are seeking to lead others. To quote Don Cousins again:

They can't effectively promote the product of spirituality unless they're involved in the daily practice of spirituality.[12]

The third area is *ministry fit*. We have already referred to the issue of passion. Another way of describing this area is to use the word 'call'. No matter how many gifts a person may have which might equip them to perform a particular ministry, unless they are convinced that they have a specific call to the ministry which would utilise these gifts, they will never be able perform well in that area.

The fourth area cited by Don Cousins is *relational fit*. It is important that leaders are able to enjoy working with those in the team with whom they need to spend time. As Cousins puts it, 'Even if we didn't work together, we'd enjoy spending time together.'[13]

The selection of the right leaders for each task is so critical to the overall task that it is well worth investing a great deal of time in making the right choices. Don Cousins refers to the ministry of Jesus as providing a model for this degree of care:

In the first year of ministry, Jesus worked with a large number of disciples. When it was time to center in on potential leaders, he went away for a night of prayer, returned, and then selected the twelve.[14]

If Jesus needed to wait a year and pray all night, shouldn't we wait to see the fruit of potential leader's lives?[15]

Willow Creek's concern to act wisely in this area is indicated
by at least three characteristics of the process that they use for
such selection.

First, *they do not appoint leaders quickly.* They always
make sure that they have observed people's behaviour over a
period of time. For this reason, many of those appointed have
already been members of the church for some time. Only if
they really cannot find those with the particular skills that they
are seeking will they recruit outside the congregation. Even
then, it is likely that they will have had a significant relationship with those that they appoint for some time already. They
tend not to appoint people with whom they have not had time
to develop relationship.

Second, *the questions that are asked in an interview situation can be very direct and specific.* We have seen in the
previous chapter an illustration of the kind of questions that
Don Cousins might ask in an interview. His concern is not to
be unnecessarily intrusive, but as he puts it, 'Why must we
discuss such basic spiritual issues? Because people who carry
the weight of leadership need to practice the fundamen-
tals... They can't effectively promote the product of spirituality unless they're involved in the daily practice of
spirituality.'[16]

Third, *a person is often given a smaller task to see how
faithfully they perform in that before they are given a larger
one.* At the same time, Willow Creek expects to challenge those
who have proved their ability to handle one task, by ensuring
that the next task contains an element of challenge so that
people are stretched. A critical element in such an approach is
to ensure that leaders also feel supported, rather than simply
left to handle the new assignment with inadequate guidance.

Don Cousins highlights a fourfold progression in the
development of those for whom he is responsible (an insight he
borrowed from Ken Blanchard's *The One Minute Manager*).
This procedure works whether the person being supervised is
an emerging leader, or someone who is a worker on a team. He
calls the four stages Direction, Coaching, Support and Delegation. Direction requires the greatest amount of input and

involves the most basic instruction. This approach would only be needed when someone was very inexperienced. Each successive stage requires less input, so that by the time the Delegation stage has been reached the person being supervised should be in a position to operate with encouragement only.

Moving from one stage to another needs to take place on the basis of a negotiated relationship. Both the new leader and the person to whom he or she is responsible need to be happy that they are operating in the appropriate stage. Clearly the speed at which people feel able to move through such a process will vary enormously from person to person and task to task, but the underlying principle remains the same.

THE TASK OF A STAFF MEMBER

Peter Wagner, in his teaching on 'breaking the 200 barrier', points to a profound change that characterises the leadership practice of larger, growing churches. Wagner notes that in the not-too-distant past, a key concept in the practice of ministry was that of being an enabler. An enabler is someone who makes room for others in the church to exercise their gifts. In more recent times ministers of larger, growing churches have tended to be trainers. They have sought not just to create space for others but also to train people to perform very specific tasks in the life of the church.

The concept of accomplishing the work of ministry through others is vital to understanding the way in which Willow Creek expects its employed staff leadership to work. Don Cousins expresses the concept this way:

> We try to teach our staff to invest their lives in people who have the potential to do one of two things: expand the staff member's circle of ministry, or replace him or her in the circle. After two or three years of training, the one being trained ought to contribute enough to free the staff member to expand the ministry or to hand it over and move on to a new endeavor.[17]

Such a concept revolutionises the way in which staff are used. In such a model, staff are not employed to run the ministry so much as to train others for ministry. There is perhaps no better example of this principle at work than the ministry of caring for the building and grounds at Willow Creek. Despite the size of the facility and campus, surprisingly there is only one staff member assigned to the upkeep of the building and grounds. Clearly it would be impossible for one person, no matter how gifted or hardworking, to manage such a task by themselves; but in fact the task is performed by the members of Willow Creek. The function of the staff person is to service the team, ensuring that the right equipment is available, recruiting and training new team members, and co-ordinating the efforts of the team.

Not only does such an approach release resources for other ministries, it also ensures that there is a way for a large number of individuals to express their unique ministry. The involvement of such large numbers of lay people, whose contribution is not just helpful but essential, allows those who share in the team to fully own the ministry, and by extension the vision, of Willow Creek.

The use of staff to act as a means of multiplying ministry rather than simply doing ministry themselves has led to the enrolment of large numbers of volunteers. The weekend children's programme, 'Promiseland', uses 1,200 volunteers every weekend. The Sonlight Express programme, designed for 11-13 year olds, receives help from 120 adult volunteers and helpers.

THE TEAM THAT LEADERS LEAD

At the beginning of this chapter we looked at the importance of a mobilised membership and noted that liberating the gift of leadership is crucial in producing that mobilisation. But we need to remember that leaders do not appear from nowhere. Generally the best leaders in a church have emerged from a pool of already mobilised members. Moreover, if even the best leaders are to lead effectively, it is essential that those they seek to lead be willing to participate in the team. To participate fully in any team, members need to be aware of their gifts and abilities. They need to know what they have to offer to the enterprise. In short, they need to be mobilised.

Most churches would appreciate the results of a mobilised membership but are often unsure how to begin such a process. Two initiatives are essential. First, it is important to help church members identify their spiritual gifts. Second, and just as important, is the development of a process whereby church members can be helped to deploy their spiritual gifts. Too many churches are adept at gift identification but do not move to this second vital stage. The result of this failure is to generate frustration on the part of members who find themselves being made aware of their gifting but are denied any avenue for service in which their gifts might be expressed. Equally, the church leadership is often perplexed because the process of gift identification does not bring the increase in mobilisation of their members that they had supposed would result.

For Willow Creek, the process of gift identification and deployment begins with their Network Serving Seminar. As with the Impact Evangelism Seminars, the course consists of four two-hour sessions and is taught on a selected night throughout a given month. Three nights are selected on a rotation basis. One month the seminar is taught on a Sunday night, the next on a Tuesday night and finally the same material is offered on a Monday night. The intention is to ensure that everyone is able to attend at least one of these evenings on a regular basis. This seminar is important enough in the development of the total programme at Willow Creek to be offered throughout the whole year with the exception of December.

It is not possible in this book to explain the content of the course in detail, but it is possible to highlight a number of vital features of this material. First, there is a conviction that underlies this material which claims that: 'PASSIONS, SPIRITUAL GIFTS, AND TEMPERAMENT work together to lead people into joy-filled, fruitful ministry.'[18] Bruce Bugbee, the compiler of the Network material, recognises that it is impossible to motivate people to fulfil someone else's vision and passion. Those who serve another person's dream can only ever see service as a duty or requirement, not necessarily as a joy. In contrast, the conviction of the Network material is expressed as follows:

> When people serve in the areas of their passions, they serve enthusiastically. They do not have motivation problems, because they are pursuing their personal dreams. When people serve according to their giftedness, they serve competently.... When people serve in ways that are consistent with their God-given temperaments, they feel free to be themselves.[19]

Second, the Network seminar material contains a great deal of biblical teaching on the subject of giftedness, but this is placed in the context of teaching on what it means to be both a servant and a steward of God's gifts. The effect of such teaching is to emphasise the importance of using abilities with a healthy attitude of service. This balance avoids the temptation to see the purpose of the church as solely a channel for the gifts of individuals. Instead, members are encouraged to see their gifts as valuable when placed at the disposal of the church. It is not always easy to convey a concept of servanthood, given both the radical individualism of Western culture and given also an emphasis on the discovery of an individual's gifts, passions and temperament. The inclusion of a strong element of self-discovery can all too easily lead to the kind of individualism that is the exact opposite of servanthood.

Third, the Network seminar is intensely practical. One of the most compelling features of the material is the way in which it uses a number of exercises to accurately identify what gifts individuals see in themselves. This information is then checked against what others observe about each person and what a person's actual experience has been. Finally, participants are encouraged to consider what they feel strongly convicted to accomplish. The same practical emphasis at the gift discovery stage is repeated at the gift deployment stage. The material groups the various spiritual gifts under a number of ministry areas. There is a list of literally hundreds of volunteer positions, printed under each main ministry area. One of the senior staff members of Willow Creek told me that he remembered how his wife had been unsure of any gifts that she might have but was transformed in her vision of what she could contribute, by the very thorough and comprehensive nature of the material covered by the Network seminar.

Fourth, each participant is encouraged to make an appointment with a lay Network counsellor who helps them to anchor their discoveries in a specific area of service. This personal ingredient ensures that the material does not remain in the area of theory. The very clear intention is that there should be a practical outcome that is realistic both in terms of a person's gifting and availability. It does not help the church or the person to have someone with considerable ability linked to an avenue of service when, in truth, they do not have the time to undertake the task in question. The counsellor helps a person to find a ministry that is appropriate in terms of every aspect of an individual's actual situation.

At the time of writing approximately 150 people attend each of these seminars. Those attending range from people who are not yet believers to those who are new Christians; it includes those who have been part of the church for a long time. The uncommitted are placed alongside those who are believers and are encouraged to see the need for a personal commitment to Christ before they are ready to offer themselves to a position of committed service. Those who have been believers for some time may already be serving in some capacity, but might feel the need to reconsider the ministry that they are currently offering. That might be because they now feel ready to give more time; or it might be that they feel that they have discovered more about themselves and are therefore ready to serve in a different area. All are welcome, no matter what stage they might be at.

THE WHOLE CHURCH MADE WHOLE

Inevitably, any organisation that enjoys a high visibility and that manages to involve large numbers of people has been shaped to a very large extent by the vision of its founders and current leaders. It can hardly be denied that the original group of leaders recruited by Bill Hybels has been critically important in the development of Willow Creek. However, it has only been possible for Willow Creek to go on growing and developing through the quality of a growing number of other leaders. These leaders are themselves able to be more effective because they are leading church members who have been properly discipled.

This significant involvement of the whole congregation is part of what we might call the rediscovery of the laity by the church in the twentieth century.

The evangelical leader Leighton Ford has pointed to such a development as a megatrend in the church of the late twentieth century, and also as a fulfilment of a process first begun in the Reformation but arrested by an overdependence on an educated, professional, clergy.[20] In the same address he noted that it has been estimated that as many as 83% of the unreached peoples of the world can only be reached by the laity because professional missionaries do not have access to those countries. It is very probable that many in our own society will only be reached when the whole church is mobilised to reach out. It is certainly the case that the church itself will only be whole when it is in a position to benefit from all of the gifts that God has liberally bestowed on all those who desire to serve him.

Willow Creek represents a model of the church which attempts to draw on all the riches that God has bestowed on his people. However, it is important to make a distinction between the exact outworking of a particular model and the principles which underlie it. The particular model which Willow Creek has developed is exciting and inspirational. It is probably also unique.

The fact that thousands of church leaders now attend the church leaders' Conferences held at Willow Creek three times a year, and that many others visit informally at other times, means that inevitably some will attempt to duplicate what Willow Creek has done. That is not the way to obtain the best from this model. A more encouraging, if more difficult, scenario would be to learn from the principles that are used by Willow Creek and then seek to contextualise those principles in a variety of other unique models. God is a creator, not the designer of a production line! The work of his hand is usually unique and not a pale carbon copy of something he has done elsewhere. However, many of us work best when we see something concrete in front of us. It is when we see the idea expressed that we are helped to understand the nature of the idea itself. Willow Creek offers itself as a working model, but it would be tragic if our knowledge of one model served to limit our creativity with regard to the principles themselves.

What follows in this book is a variety of models, most of which came into being with no knowledge of Willow Creek. The intention of describing these models is to encourage an exploration of the principles common to all of them, in the hope that many more expressions of a church for the unchurched will come into being.

FOOTNOTES

1. For more detail on this research see R. Pointer, *How Do Churches Grow* (Marc Europe: 1984), p 102f.

2. M. Robinson and S. Christine, *Planting Tomorrow's Churches Today* (Monarch: 1992), p 207ff.

3. John Finney, *Understanding Leadership* (DLT: 1989), p 35.

4. *Ibid.*

5. Eddie Gibbs, *Followed or Pushed* (Marc: 1987), p 21.

6. Don Cousins, *Mastering Church Management* (Multnomah Press: 1990), p 77.

7. *Ibid*, p 114.

8. *Ibid*, p 113.

9. *Ibid*, p 114.

10. *Ibid*, p 118.

11. *Ibid.*

12. *Ibid*, p 121.

13. *Ibid*, p 122.

14. Luke 6:12–16 and Mark 3:13–19.

15. Don Cousins, *op cit*, p 124.

16. *Ibid*, p 120f.

17. *Ibid*, p 117.

18. Bruce Bugbee, *Network Serving Seminar Handbook*, p 4b.

19. *Ibid.*

20. Leighton Ford, 'The World We Live In', Address to the Evangelists Conference, Swanwick, Dec. 1989.

CHAPTER NINE

On the Waterfront

A BOVE BAR CHURCH has a long history as a good-sized evangelical congregation set in the centre of Southampton. The attention of Christians in other parts of Britain was drawn to Above Bar by its inclusion in the book *Ten Growing Churches*.[1] In that book we learn that the congregation was begun in 1876 by an American evangelist, Henry Earl, who was church planting on behalf of a movement known as Churches of Christ. Early in the twentieth century, the Above Bar congregation severed its connections with Churches of Christ and later became a congregation within the Fellowship of Independent Evangelical Churches. It saw dramatic growth during the 1980s under the leadership of David Jackman. In 1978 attendance was around 400. By 1990 close to 1,000 different people attended one or other of the three Sunday services at Above Bar. The congregation included people from all parts of the city.

As you might expect from this kind of growth, David Jackman was always looking for new ways in which to bring people to an awareness of the person of Christ. He had heard of the church at Willow Creek and began to wonder if it might be possible to hold an event at Above Bar that would specifically target the unchurched. In the autumn of 1989 the church held a six-week series of presentations about the Christian faith. Christians were encouraged to bring their unchurched friends. It was held at eight o'clock on a Sunday evening after the regular Sunday evening worship had finished. A number of the staff members at Above Bar contributed to this event as well as David Jackman. They were delighted by the response; both Christians and their interested friends attended.

Success brings its own problems. In this case the immediate problem was to know what to do next. They decided to hold a second series in the spring of 1990 which would essentially build on the first series. In order to assist the presentation, they felt that it would be helpful if the regular evening service could be moved forward slightly to create more space for the evangelistic after-event. The request to move the evening service brought some unexpected resistance within the church at Above Bar. The effect of that debate was to raise a question about the long-term future for a 'seeker-sensitive' or 'seeker-targeted' event within the church context. While the church had a commitment to evangelism, the need for radical new approaches to reach totally unchurched people was not accepted by some. Older Christians, who had many years of church life behind them, found it hard to appreciate how alienated from conventional forms of services a whole generation of unchurched people really is.

By that time, however, there was a small group of people who had caught the vision and who were not willing to let it go so easily. One of those who had seen the potential for such an event was Trevor Waldock, one of the staff members at Above Bar. Trevor had made a Christian commitment while in his mid-teens as a result of a special evangelistic event held in a barn. He had not previously had strong connections with any church and might not have heard a compelling presentation of the Christian message had he not attended this 'seeker-sensitive' event intended for non-Christians.

Following his conversion, Trevor went to work at a Capernwray project in Austria primarily using his skills as a teacher in the area of youth work. While he was there he felt a strong calling to come back to England and work as a missionary among his own people. After a time as a pastor's assistant serving a church in Cambridgeshire, and then a period as a teaching elder in a church in Essex, Trevor joined the staff of Above Bar in 1987 specifically to work in the field of training.

To some extent, Trevor had always struggled to fit into church life. Apart from some exposure to Sunday school he had neither been brought up in a church nor converted in a church. Consequently he had always felt slightly outside the culture of church life. As he reflected on the autumn and spring series at Above Bar in which he had participated, he began to wonder if his own experiences might be a helpful background for someone who wanted to reach the unchurched.

WESTSIDE STORY

If the existing congregation at Above Bar was not ready to absorb the new vision, why not try locating it in a new congregation? It so happened that Above Bar had recently begun a new work in another part of Southampton which they had called the Westside congregation.

As we have noted Above Bar drew its members and attenders from all parts of the city; it ran house groups in many parts of Southampton. Three of those house groups were situated in a district which, as the name suggests, lay on the West side of the city. For several years they had gradually developed a vision for their own congregation to serve that specific part of the city. They also needed a minister. Trevor Waldock was already on the staff of the sponsoring church and was looking for an appropriate means by which to fulfil his vision for reaching the unchurched. What better solution than to invite Trevor to pastor the new work?

The first step was to engage in some survey work, both to gauge the degree of openness on the part of unchurched people and to see what kinds of issue they were concerned about. Fortunately, Trevor was able to draw on the services of a number of Americans who were spending the summer in Britain working with Above Bar in voluntary Christian work.

The survey results were both helpful and encouraging and an attempt was made to begin outreach during the autumn of 1990.

However, it soon became clear that there were some differences of view within the leadership. Although there had been an initial agreement in the spring of that year, it emerged that there were differing views on leadership and strategy within the leadership group. Some of the Westside congregation did not really have the same priority for reaching the unchurched that Trevor had, though they certainly wanted to see growth and were prepared to see anyone who was unchurched become a Christian and join their church. After six months, Trevor felt that he needed to withdraw from the congregation at Westside and return to Above Bar to rethink his situation.

FRESH INSPIRATION

After he had withdrawn from the work at Westside, Trevor returned to Above Bar and continued on the staff at the mother church. During this time he was involved in teaching Christian Basics courses to enquirers at Above Bar. In addition, he took responsibility for running another two mini-series similar to the earlier experimental events. This time they took the themes of 'How to let your marriage fall apart without even knowing', and 'Suffering'. While this was all successful to some extent, Trevor was becoming increasingly convinced of the need for a different context in which to locate such an enterprise. By then it had become clear that David Jackman would soon be moving into a new training ministry. Trevor began to consider his options. He saw three clear alternatives. He could obtain a secular job and remain in Southampton; he could look for a ministry elsewhere; or he could try again to launch a project which targetted the unchurched seeker.

This process of reflection was aided by Trevor's attendance at a Willow Creek leadership conference which was held in Paris for European church leaders. Trevor was now able to see the model in more detail and to reflect on how it might be transferred to a European context. Willow Creek therefore offered a fully developed strategy for a concept that until then had lacked a coherent framework in which a concern for the unchurched could be fully expressed. In addition, Trevor had met Jerry Butler from Willow Creek, who had encouraged him to consider beginning something similar to Willow Creek in an English context.

During his first year at Southampton–and more specifically while at Westside–Trevor had formed a strong friendship with Rob Poole, a local businessman. Rob had become a Christian at Above Bar as a previously unchurched adult and felt very drawn to the kind of vision that Trevor had for a different kind of church, one designed to meet the needs of the unchurched people that Rob met in his business life. He was only too aware that very few of his business friends would feel comfortable in the context of the normal church service at Westside or Above Bar. A different kind of context was needed. Both Rob and Trevor felt instinctively that they had much to learn from the Willow Creek model.

With all this ferment in mind, Rob and Trevor accepted an invitation to attend a church leader's conference at Willow Creek in May 1991. Their purpose in attending this event was not just to see Willow Creek for themselves or even to reflect further on the model, but to obtain as much information as possible with a view to actually implementing something of what they saw. Whereas Trevor's visit to the Paris conference had introduced him to a strategy for reaching the unchurched, the experience at Willow Creek gave them exposure to a working mission model from which they could learn very concrete lessons.

Both Rob and Trevor returned from the Willow Creek conference convinced that this model could work in England, and even more convinced that they wanted to try it. The only remaining question for them was whether Above Bar church would respond favourably to such a proposal or whether they might need to find some other way of bringing such a vision into being.

A NEW CORE GROUP

During their visit to the United States, Trevor and Rob worked on developing some very uncompromising proposals to put to the church at Above Bar. Trevor describes the proposals as a 'clean sheet or bust'.[2] They decided to ask Above Bar for the freedom to recruit at least forty people from the congregation for a new work. Further, they wanted the church to continue to provide Trevor with a salary for a year and to allow complete freedom for them to develop an appropriate style of congregation for reaching the unchurched. Having witnessed some of the tensions at Above Bar over the earlier proposals for existing innovative forms of evangelism, they were anxious that the new work would not be governed by the existing congregation. They believed that it would be necessary to form a congregation that would be strongly directed by the leadership. Willow Creek provided both a model and an inspiration for this new work.

Even though Trevor and Rob were both excited by their visit to Willow Creek and were perhaps ready to aim for more than they might otherwise have done, neither of them felt over-optimistic about the reception that their proposals would receive. Faith was tempered by a feeling of being 'gutted' by their earlier false start. But in fact they arrived back from Chicago on a Monday morning in May and by the Thursday of the same week had obtained agreement from Above Bar's leaders for everything that they had asked. They were surprised and delighted; this was the confirmation they had sought.

The core group that they desired to recruit came together rather easily over the summer months. They were by now clear that the group that they wished to target would be young professionals in their twenties and thirties, many of whom would be singles or young marrieds without children. The core group met twice over the summer months at Above Bar so that strategy could be explained.

The four months from September to December were used to build the core group's understanding of what they were trying to accomplish. The earlier experience at WestSide and what they had learnt at Willow Creek taught them that it was important to communicate strategy, vision and values to the core group. The strategy and vision were perhaps the easiest to communicate to a group of people who had all been recruited on the basis of a desire to reach the unchurched. The issue of the central values of the group was much more difficult to communicate, if only because values are seen most clearly in the practical exercise of ministry.

The group met every Wednesday throughout the autumn period. This preparatory time was essential not just in terms of helping the group to get to know each other and to communicate information, but even more importantly the launch was only really going to work if the people in the core group were ready to invite their friends. It was therefore essential to both train and build confidence in those who were going to be inviting others. The function of the core group was emphatically not just to fill enough seats so that the building would look respectably full; this was to be a working team. Recruits were needed to form a drama group and to help with the technical production, music and set-up. Four months were only just long enough to prepare for what was to come.

PREPARING THE GROUND

During the autumn at least one unforseen and seemingly insurmountable problem emerged. Neither Rob nor Trevor was gifted in music and programme planning. It quickly became clear that they needed a 'point person' to head up these two vital and related areas.

During the time that this problem was being considered, Jerry Butler and Lee Strobel visited Great Britain and were able to spend time with Trevor. The problem was discussed in some detail. During their deliberations it emerged that Trevor did know the ideal person to head up certainly the music aspect of the project. However, the person concerned – Andy Silver – was already working for Above Bar, and it became clear that if they were to approach him, they would need to undertake to find a salary for him very soon after they launched. On the other hand, Trevor was convinced that Andy had a vision for reaching the unchurched. The counsel of the visitors from Willow Creek was to attempt to recruit the right person from the beginning. To Trevor's delight Andy agreed to join the team, but the decision to come was not finally made until the middle of December, just a few short weeks before the launch date.

The time-pressure that Trevor's total commitment to the new project imposed upon him suggested to them that it would be wiser for the new group to take responsibility for his salary as soon as they launched, even though Above Bar had agreed to continue with the salary arrangements for a full year. This meant that it was necessary to make some adjustments to their budget plans. Andy would join the paid staff very soon afterwards, with Above Bar helping until then.

To add to their last-minute problems, the person that they had planned to use as a singer was unable to help them, and this did not become clear until very near the launch date. Their imagination, ingenuity and faith were tested while they searched for a good replacement. Just a few weeks before and after the launch, Andy was able to find four soloists, one of whom was the wife of an Anglican vicar who lived some miles from Southampton. These singers have been an important part of the team especially during the early week of the launch.

Apart from the matter of the team members, the most critical problem was to find the right place to meet. The process of looking for the right premises helped to further define the nature of the project. It quickly became clear that they wanted a city-centre venue, because they knew that they would be attempting to draw people from all over the city. This was not to be a community church which would target everyone in a given locality. Instead, they were seeking young professionals wherever they might live in the city. They were also aware that the city centre was 'familiar territory' for the kind of target group that they had in mind.

The question of when they might meet would also affect where they could meet. Their knowledge of their own group, together with their earlier experiences at Above Bar, tended to suggest that later on a Sunday evening would be a good time to reach the target group that they had in mind.

But what kind of building would be suitable? It was clear from the beginning that they did not want to rent a church building, even if one should be available on a Sunday night. Cinemas are not easily available for rent on a Sunday evening. At a fairly early stage, Trevor was convinced that the Novotel, a new and prominent city centre hotel, offered a good venue. Car parking was good, it was easy for people coming in to the city to find and the facilities were excellent. Even more important, hotels are not busy on a Sunday night and so were glad to offer attractive rates for someone wanting to rent a function room for one night every week of the year!

Although they did not make the decision immediately, and in the meantime continued to look for other premises, it was the Novotel option that they eventually adopted. The deciding factor was simply the realisation that this was a setting where the unchurched people whom they were seeking to reach would feel very comfortable. For many of these people, hotels very similar to the Novotel were places where they often stayed overnight in connection with work. It was somewhere where business was often conducted. The restaurant and function rooms were all designed with the business community in mind. This really was the church going out to meet the unchurched where they were!

JUST LOOKING

Having found the right place, what was the service going to look like? Would it be a direct copy of a Willow Creek Seeker's Service? If not, in what respects would it be different, and why? The feeling of Trevor and Rob was that the unchurched people whom they were seeking to reach in Britain were even more unfamiliar with church worship than were unchurched people in Chicago. They therefore designed a one-hour format that did not call for any participation from the audience. They put together a five-month programme featuring five major themes, most of which broke down into four or five topics.

They decided to call it 'Just Looking' and designed attractive brochures and ancillary material to give an identity to the overall presentation.

The next step was to begin to accumulate equipment. They needed a good sound and lighting system; such equipment is rarely cheap. The core group had already begun to give to the project before the launch, and some £6,000 was raised before Christmas in order to buy the necessary equipment. Such generous giving helped to lay a helpful foundation for the budget that they would need once the launch took place.

As the various ingredients for the 'Just Looking' event came together, and as the time for the launch drew near, rehearsals were essential. At this point they discovered something of the extent of the task that they had taken on. Even with a good-sized, highly proficient and committed team, they found that it took around three hours to set up the equipment, test it all, pray, and rehearse the various ingredients. All too soon, the day that they had all been praying towards arrived.

THE POST-LAUNCH EXPERIENCE

The launch date for the first 'Just Looking' was 5 January 1992. By the time that this date drew near, the original core group of fifty-five had grown; there was another group of friends, who although not part of the core group, were not all strictly part of the target group either. Among them were unchurched people who were supportive of what was happening. This meant that they could be fairly sure of at least eighty people on the first night.

In the event, only just over eighty came. Although this aspect of the launch was slightly disappointing, nothing else was. They were pleased that the event came together in the way that they had envisaged. It was a success in that it gave the core group and their friends the confidence to go out and invite others for the next week. Everyone now felt convinced that this was a quality event which would not embarrass anyone. The second week around 120 people came, of whom about forty were unchurched people. Although the occasional week was down a little and some weeks were over this total, the numbers over the first few months stayed around that number. However, it was not all the same people who came back week after week. Some who were 'just looking' came to look and didn't come back. Those people were replaced by yet other unchurched people.

What do these events feel like to an attender? The content of each week's programme is slightly different but includes a mixture of drama, contemporary music, interviews with those who have become Christians, and a half-hour 'message' on the chosen subject for that evening. At the beginning of the evening the lights go down and do not go up again until the end of the one-hour presentation. During that time, the audience do not participate to any greater extent than an audience would at a performace in a theatre. The 'message' style is informal, almost like a blend of chat show and the kind of studied, serious, yet engaging style used to present serious issues in television documentaries or Open University courses on television. As you would expect, there is no charge, as the brochure makes clear; neither is the audience asked to contribute to an offering. It would be possible for someone to come in and to leave without anyone intercepting them, although in practice virtually everyone comes because someone else has brought them.

The one problem in providing anonymity to those who attend is the danger of appearing unfriendly. It also raises the issue of the need to think through how someone is encouraged to continue on through the process, to the point where they might be ready to make some kind of a decision.

Two ingredients are vital. First, as we have already noted, each major theme is divided into a number of topics. The effect of the series approach is to encourage those who have been challenged to want to finish the series. Second, the place of friendship is important. There is an expectation that those who have brought people will continue the conversation around the specific issues that were raised by the presentation.

Just as at Willow Creek, the core group meets mid-week for worship and teaching. At the time of writing this takes place at

Above Bar, although the venue is likely to change. Unchurched people are not encouraged to come to this meeting. Instead, there is a meeting for enquirers. After two months, five people had been converted and approximately ten people were in enquirers groups.

HOPE AND EXPECTATION

The experiment at 'Just Looking' is in its very early days at the time of writing and many changes may take place during the first year of its operation. However, even at this stage it is clear that some of the core concepts are attracting sufficient interest for the group to be confident that their vision for reaching the unchurched can be fulfilled. They are realistic enough not to expect dramatic growth, especially in the first year. The leadership in particular is committed to a process, and there is a recognition that the process is a slow one, especially at first.

Some lessons are being learnt already. For example, they have discovered that the themes are crucial in terms of attracting people. Their first theme, which picked up on the question of direction in relation to the start of a New Year, was clearly a positive one. They feared that attendance would drop significantly as soon as the second series started, because the titles centred around Jesus. In fact the numbers were maintained. It is not that their preaching ignores Jesus, far from it. But experience has shown that a consideration of the person of Jesus for the unchurched is best done in the context of looking at what Trevor calls 'people life issues'.

It is also clear that radical and different approaches to 'doing church' involves some risk-taking. Not too long after their launch, the local press carried an article which described them as a church in a bar. This was not strictly accurate; although there is a bar outside the function room where they meet, that is not where the 'Just Looking' presentations take place. However, such an article did not meet with the approval of every member at Above Bar, some of whom were conscious that the publicity made a link between 'Just Looking' and Above Bar. However, whether accurate or not, there is a good chance that the unchurched did notice it. At the very least, the team at Southampton can be pleased they are not being ignored by those they seek to reach.

FOOTNOTES

1. Eddie Gibbs (ed), *Ten Growing Churches* (MARC Europe: 1984).

2. Conversation with the author.

CHAPTER TEN

Saturday Night Church

WHAT FOLLOWS IN THIS CHAPTER is considerably more speculative than any of the other case studies in this book. One could argue that it might be unwise to say anything about these ideas because they are untried and therefore untested. If they should go badly wrong then it might later seem foolish to have written about them at all. I have rejected such reasoning because the value of ideas does not lie in whether or not they are especially successful (although one hopes that they will be), so much as in their capability to stimulate the imagination and creativity of others. It would be possible for someone to take an idea that has worked well in one place only to find that it is inappropriate elsewhere; just as another person might be able to take a concept that did not work well in one place, only to find that it was just the right idea for another situation.

In the case of the second example given in this chapter, the difficulties that were encountered were such that the project has had to be 'put on ice' for the time being. However, it can be helpful to see that not all creative ideas are easy to implement. We need to see the difficulties that can come with innovation, if only to encourage others to embrace their own creative ideas with a healthy dose of realism.

1. REACHING EUROPE'S CITY PAGANS

Geoff Crocker works in church growth ministry through itin-
erant and published Bible teaching in many parts of the world,
but also earns his living as an industrial consultant, a profession that gives him a profoundly European perspective, as
opposed to a purely British view of culture and the gospel. His
major clients are usually French or German companies whose
interests are often spread across Eastern and Western Europe.
Apart from being capable in French and German his exposure
to, and interest in, the major cities of Europe has given him an
interest in strategies which might significantly impact those
who, in their daily lives, operate with a thoroughly secular
mind-set and yet are also asking some important religious
questions about values and meaning.

Geoff was brought up in a home where the dominant ideology of his father was that of a strong working-class socialism
which rejected all religious explanations of life. His father was
far from pleased when his son, who clearly had a promising
educational future, embraced Christianity in his mid-teens.
Geoff's practical experience in evangelism was given significant encouragement when in his late teens and early twenties
he joined St Philip and St Jacob's ('Pip and Jay') Church in
Bristol, whose minister, Malcolm Widdecombe, was then
becoming well known in the emerging Charismatic renewal.

Over the past twenty years, Geoff has lived in various parts
of the British Isles, moving to live near Bristol a few years ago.
His friendships with other church leaders have included those
in the worldwide Anglican Renewal movement but have also
extended to those who are part of what used to be called the
'house church' movement (now more usually called the 'new
churches'), and others in the Baptist and Brethren movement.
His entrepreneurial skills have been put to good use in the
formation, promotion and editing of *Living Word*, a teaching
magazine which is circulated widely in Britain, continental
Europe and some other parts of the world. Geoff is currently
working on a project for a 'Saturday night church'. Although it
has not yet been launched, the concept is well advanced. It can

therefore be described here in sufficient detail to allow us to reflect upon it.

The context in which the idea was born is important if we are to obtain a feel for what Geoff is hoping to achieve. He recalls that in the autumn of 1990 he was speaking at a congregation in Liverpool known as 'City Church'. On the Saturday evening he and Len Grates, one of the leaders of the church, went to eat at a restaurant near Liverpool city centre. While in the centre, they noticed how many other people were around. Many were queuing outside some of the many new pubs and clubs that had opened in that part of the city in the mid to late 1980s.

Geoff was sufficiently intrigued by what he saw to suggest that they go in to one of the pubs to see what was happening. He noticed that there was a good mix of age groups and some mix of the kinds of people who were around. The predominant feel was that these people were at least a little affluent even if not especially wealthy. The pub was a pleasant place, tastefully if simply decorated. The whole area had a slightly expectant buzz. It reminded Geoff of many city centre scenes that he had witnessed in various cities in Europe on Saturday nights. Geoff turned to his companion and, thinking of Christian witness, said 'We should be here, now.'

Behind them stood an empty warehouse which happened to be owned by a Christian businessman. The City Church, whose vision was to reach the people of the city, was only too aware that when they met in the city centre on a Sunday morning the centre was deserted, many of the city's inhabitants being asleep in bed. It had occurred to the City Church leaders that they might use a building such as the empty warehouse, but for various reasons no proposal had yet proved viable.

Not long after this encounter, Geoff heard of Willow Creek through the author of this book. He made a connection in his mind between what Willow Creek were doing and his Saturday night experience in Liverpool. That creative moment had not been forgotten. He began to wonder if the idea might not take root in Bristol—a city which, as an historic trading port, had much in common with Liverpool. Parts of Bristol City Centre had been redeveloped to produce much the same kind of atmosphere as the part of Liverpool that he had visited. In particular, the Arnolfini centre in Bristol had been opened as a cultural centre with a mixed programme of the arts ranging from exhibitions to films and live performances. In many ways, Arnolfini was a secular model for what Geoff envisaged as a centre for Christian outreach.

The next step was to phone the planning department of the City Council to see what property might be available for redevelopment. This he did in the January of 1991. By the end of February he received an encouraging response and began to contact some Christian leaders in Bristol to test his concept with others. Geoff composed a three-page paper outlining the concept and mailed it in early May to Rob Scott Cook (a Bristol church leader), Steve Abbott (Fellowship of the King), Dave Day (Bristol Christian Fellowship), and Anthony Bush, an Anglican layman whom he had known since his Pip and Jay days. Each of them responded favourably and, together with their wives, they have acted as an oversight group for the project as it has begun to emerge. Leaders of Youth With a Mission (YWAM) across Europe have also responded with interest to the core vision. British YWAM have expressed interest in making a working contribution to the operational team.

SOLID BONES

The idea was born. It had received significant affirmation from other Christian leaders who were both spiritually mature and supportive personally of Geoff. However, even though Geoff has a very practical streak in his personality, it was important to involve others who could give the concept a solid framework. Anthony Bush reminded Geoff of a meeting that had taken place in a city centre church some months earlier. A Christian engineer, Hugh Pratt, who through establishing an engineering business in the city harbour had developed a good relationship with the planning authorities, had given his testimony. Would Hugh be interested in helping with the project? To Geoff's delight, he was. Not only was he prepared to help, but his own business was situated in a building which was very similar to the building that had been proposed as a possible location by the city planning department. Hugh had redeveloped this warehouse in much the same way that would be necessary for a Saturday night church, or Christian Arnolfini, project.

At the time of writing, negotiations are proceeding between the planning department and the group that Geoff has brought together. If all goes well, it might be possible to think in terms of a launch during 1993. If for some reason it proves not to be possible to proceed with the building that has so far been envisaged as the project's base, it is conceivable that the same concept could be developed using a different venue. Should negotiations be successful, it will be necessary to engage in some significant fund raising. One possibility is that thriving churches in countries like Singapore may well contribute some mission funding. The world of missions has moved some way since urban Europe funded rural mission in Africa and Asia!

ENFLESHING THE BONES

The building divides naturally into two sections. One section amounting to about one-third of the total is suited to development as offices, seminar rooms and possibly even as some accommodation which could house a centre manager. The remaining two-thirds could be left as a large open space where all kinds of activities could be staged. What is in Geoff Crocker's mind at this time? His hope is that such a centre could be used for a wide range of activities, perhaps with very different groups using it at different times of the week. It might be possible to have a youth-orientated event on a Friday night. A restaurant might feature on other nights. Seminars at lunch time could combine with the offer of inexpensive and simple meals. Occasional large-scale events, such as concerts or theatre productions, could also be booked. It is also possible that a congregation might want to meet there for Sunday worship with a separate youth-oriented group meeting on Sunday evenings. The basic goal would be to find as many creative uses for the building throughout the week as possible, with the central thrust being that these uses would be planned with the unchurched in mind.

Geoff describes the ambience that he is aiming for as being akin to that of a Virgin Atlantic jumbo—neat but friendly. He is convinced that such a format has the potential to appeal to everyone from the grandmother to the businessman. The relaxed but competent and comfortable presentation should put people at their ease.

But what about Saturday nights? Geoff's present vision is to put together a regular programme which would be a mixture of cabaret—featuring an excellent Christian music and drama presentation—and chat show. He says that 'Jesus would be a chat show host if he were here today.' The hope would be to draw people in, perhaps by offering food near the entrance, and to structure the event in such a way that people could wander in and out while remaining anonymous. A spoken message would be offered as a kind of 'Thought for the Day' spot.

For Geoff, the support of churches across the city is important, not just to help in the practical launch of the project, but because he sees a large element of the vision as resourcing the church throughout Bristol; partly by offering something that few if any churches could do by themselves, and partly because of the need to place potential converts in churches nearer their own home. To meet this need, Geoff proposes a kind of 'pizza menu' of churches around the city. In other words, the basic ingredient of the pizza is the gospel, but the actual form or expression of the gospel comes in a number of flavours. A menu of churches would indicate their characteristics: whether they are 'hot and spicy' or come with just a 'plain topping'. Although he describes this element with something of a twinkle in his eye, the need to place people in appropriate churches is a serious concern.

At this stage, there is still some thinking to do in terms of how initial interest might be followed up or how to encourage those who wander in either to stay or to come back on another occasion. The invitation by friends is not part of anything that Geoff has so far expressed and it may be that this ingredient will need to be further thought through. Moreover, it will also be necessary to recruit a 'core group' who will have a vision for the basic goals of the project and who would be prepared to finance the running costs, offer staffing on a voluntary basis for some of the activities, and form a good part of the audience when holding events. It may well be that once such a core has been recruited the friendship element will easily and naturally develop.

Not everyone walks around the city centre on a Saturday night. Geoff is well aware that many unchurched people are in their own homes at that time, usually watching television. So regional TV would be investigated and harnessed, as a means of drawing unchurched people to a high-profile event which isn't actually church.

Would such a concept work? It is not entirely new. The Jesus Centre in Birmingham which was established to service the converts that came out of the work of Arthur Blessit in the early 1970s had some of the same ideas connected with it. Although the Jesus Centre eventually closed its doors, it did do valuable work for a time, and what is being proposed in Bristol is both more sophisticated and for a much broader audience. By taking on board the lessons that have been learnt from others involved in working with the unchurched it is possible that this could offer a useful model, not so much for villages and small towns but for larger city conurbations. If the Bristol project does succeed then it is not unreasonable to think that such a model could spread into other major city centres throughout Europe. With his working knowledge of such cities, Geoff Crocker could well be God's agent for realising just such a vision.

2. CABARET FOR CHRIST

A second idea for a Saturday night church has sprung from a group of Christians in one of England's newly expanding towns. It is not so ambitious as the plans of Geoff Crocker and has the potential to be operated either by one church on its own or by a group of churches. As I have indicated at the beginning of this chapter, for a number of reasons this basic idea has not yet been put into operation, so the actual church concerned is not identified here.

The fundamental concept centres around four basic ingredients, most of which have been identified already and occasionally acted upon by the same church. What are these ingredients? first is *the conviction that unchurched people may be willing to attend quality events which present some aspect of the Christian message in a context that feels significantly different from a worship event.* The church's feeling is that all worship services demand something from those who attend, even if that 'something' is only to stand at the right points in the service and attempt to sing unfamiliar words to unknown tunes. The basic ingredients of the proposed event would be music, possibly drama, a kind of hosted chat show presentation, and finally some kind of challenging message that attempts to relate the Christian faith to life issues.

A second ingredient is *the observation that before it is possible to plan a programme for such an event it is essential to attempt to discover the 'felt needs' of the target group.* All too often Christians assume that they know what concerns non-Christians have without really making much attempt to research that area. As some pundits put it, 'Christians are sure that Jesus is the answer, but they have forgotten the question.' In reality, very little research—if any—has been undertaken into what concerns occupy the minds of the unchurched. What is clear from the little that we do know is that the issues that are important to unchurched people cannot be assumed to be universally the same. Differences in social class, age and regional variations all combine to influence the kind of approach that would be necessary to touch the concerns of the target group.

A third element is *a commitment to high-quality publicity.* Although the precise format and content of any leaflets and other printed materials would depend to some extent on the issues that were being highlighted, the intention that quality design and production should be utilised remains constant whatever the theme. Well-designed invitations and programmes need also to be supplemented by other forms of publicity and particularly local press coverage. It is not that such impersonal forms of communication have a direct impact in terms of bringing people to an event, but they do provide a helpful context in which a personal invitation can be offered.

That brings us to the fourth ingredient, which is *the simple recognition that personal invitations to friends, neighbours and relatives are the most effective means of bringing unchurched people to an event.* The church that we are describing is one which has already built some significant relationships with unchurched people, some of which have been developed by means of occasional evangelistic events somewhat similar to the Saturday night concept.

With such a well-developed plan already in operation and with a fairly successful track record of occasional evangelistic events, why hasn't the concept of Saturday night church taken off in this context? All the right ingredients seem to be in place—what else is required? The church recognised the very considerable amount of hard work that would be required to make this approach work. They were more than willing to invest their time and energy in helping to realise such a concept. The stumbling block was not their willingness to work comprehensively towards their goal but rather an unforeseen obstacle in relation to the second ingredient listed above. When they attempted to conduct research into the 'felt needs' of their target group, they found it almost impossible to obtain enough co-operation from those whom they approached to arrive at a satisfactory research outcome.

The method that they used was to go door-to-door with a survey designed to discover the concerns of people in their target area. In practice they discovered that people simply turned them away. These were not questions that people on the doorsteps were prepared to answer, possibly because the attempt to do so required more thinking effort than they were really prepared to expend on behalf of strangers. It became clear that the church would need to obtain their research data in some other way or to be prepared to invest more time and energy in the survey work. The experience was a little disheartening for those who took part.

In the meantime, the church had attempted a rather different strategy in its evangelism programme. They had begun to call door-to-door, but this time instead of asking for help with their survey they were asking those whom they called on whether they knew of any needs (either their own or others) that the church might pray for (an example of this kind of calling can be found in a Grove Booklet by Martin Robinson, *'Door to Door' Calling*). The response was dramatically better than anything that they had encountered in their survey work; or in other door to door evangelistic activity; so much better, in fact, that some who had expressed reservations about the type of door to door calling because of earlier negative experiences began to want to take part.

Needless to say, for the moment at least, the much more complex and long-term project of a Saturday night church has been laid aside in favour of the prayer strategy which is receiving a warm response from unchurched people. What can we learn from all this? Certainly it is important to stay flexible. It is pointless to become just as doctrinaire by attempting to insist that one particular way of reaching the unchurched is the only proper way and that no other way will do. We cannot tell unchurched people that there are tried and tested means by which they should come to Christ, and that they really ought to follow those channels!

We need to be sensitive also to what we are realistically able to accomplish at any one time. On occasions, a few visionary people in a church will see the potential for a particular project, and they may well be right, but either their church just cannot cope with the project, or unforeseen obstacles block the way. It would be wiser to be a little patient, to concentrate instead on plans that their church *can* accomplish, and to wait until the time is right to implement the original vision.

Other responses might include the possibility of co-operating with other churches in a venture that is too much for one church to manage; or even to consider occasional, or at most monthly, events which it might be possible to tackle immediately. A passionate desire to reach the unchurched needs to be both creative and practical: creative enough to see the potential for new ways of being the church for the unchurched, and practical enough to find ways of adapting the vision to the resources and opportunities that God has put at our disposal.

CHAPTER ELEVEN

Innovation in the Dales

A HEART FOR THE UNCHURCHED

WHEN JOHN LEWIS first left school, his horizons were very far indeed from the hills of the Yorkshire Dales. In Christian circles, the word 'navigator' conjures up an image of someone engaged in personal witnessing, particularly on student campuses. John Lewis was a navigator in the maritime sense of the word, which meant that he spent most of his working life navigating oil tankers across the major oceans of the world.

He was not a Christian when he first went to sea, and you might think that life on board a ship was not a very likely environment for someone to encounter the Christian faith. More often than not you would be correct, but John had some good friends he had known at school, some of whom had become Christians. A few of these friends wrote to John to tell him of their Christian experience and also sent him tapes to listen to. As you might imagine, there was not a great deal for John to do on board ship outside his work schedule, so he spent time listening to the tapes. In time he became a Christian while still at sea and far removed from any church context.

Maintaining his Christian commitment while on board ship was not easy, but he was able to do so, albeit with some struggles. Later he felt called to go to Bible College with a longer-term view to some kind of Christian service. Perhaps if he had been in a local church he might have received advice to attend one or other of the denominationally-linked colleges. The absence of any church connection, combined with other factors, led him to attend Faith Mission Bible College in Edinburgh. The college had been linked to a particular branch of the holiness movement which had been involved in the Hebridean revival.

Unusual as it was for an Englishman to attend a Scottish college, he set about his studies with great vigour and learnt many lessons in relation to the unchurched which helped to shape his thinking. One of his favourite stories concerns his attempt to sell the college magazine, entitled *Life Indeed*. Students from the college attempted to sell this publication in various public houses in Edinburgh. John was given the task of selling it on the docks of Leith. He quickly discovered that not many sailors were interested in reading about the life of holiness! Undeterred, he began to think about how he might communicate with his target audience. He hit on the idea of forming a music group to capture the attention of his potential clients. Having got this far he approached the manager of one of the clubs frequented by sailors. The manager told him that he could go on between the acts, most of which were 'go-go' dancers.

He found that this approach enabled him to talk to people. Eventually he became known by the regulars in the local clubland fraternity. He remembers very well an incident when a local prostitute was badly beaten. John and the team visited her there. He recalled her words: 'You people are different. You bring the church to us.' It has been this quest to 'bring the church to us', that has played a formative part in the evangelistic motivation of John Lewis.

RENEWING THE WINESKINS

Following his time at Faith Mission Bible College during the early 1980s John became involved in what was then one of the fastest-growing Methodist churches in Britain, South Chadderton (Oldham), in Manchester. The church was near his parent's home and he became vitally involved in the evangelistic outreach of the church. While there he learnt a good deal about the theory of Church Growth which Eddie Gibbs of the Bible Society had begun to teach. From there he accepted a call to be trained for the Baptist ministry and studied at Northern Baptist College in Manchester, at the same time having a student pastorate. The student pastorate allowed him to meet his wife Mandy and together they arrived in June 1986 to begin a ministry with Skipton Baptist Church.

Skipton had been an old cotton town and was experiencing something of a renewal because of the booming tourist trade. The town calls itself the 'gateway to the Dales', and the Dales were becoming a popular location for visitors from Britain and elsewhere, partly because of the over-popularity of the Lake District and partly through the writing of James Herriot. This was classic Herriot country and was promoted as such. The town itself has a population of 12,000, most of whom have been born and brought up in the general area. Some 'incomers' from other parts of Britain have bought cottages and other farm buildings in the area around the town. A few have moved to the town itself.

The Baptist church is well located, although it is not as easily noticed from the main thoroughfares as some of the other church buildings in the town. The congregation was begun in Skipton in the nineteenth century, so it was not really a recent church plant even for a well-settled area. When John and Mandy arrived, a typical congregation consisted of some forty or fifty people, most of whom, though not all, were senior citizens.

Their priority was to discover how to create an environment in which unchurched people could feel comfortable. John was aware that in the holiday season Skipton was crowded with visitors from all over the world, some of whom might appreciate a warm and friendly worship service. Perhaps if he could attract some of these visitors, the church would look fuller and livelier, and it might also have a wider range of age groups in the congregation. Even though none of these visitors would become a permanent part of the congregation, the continued presence of different visitors in the congregation would help to create the environment that he needed if they were going to attract the unchurched people who actually lived in the town.

With this in mind, John had a very attractive card printed. It was well designed, with a mixture of the same contemporary and yet historic image that characterised so much else in this revitalised tourist town. He ensured that every guest house and hotel in the immediate area had ample copies available for their guests. The following Sunday, some forty visitors came to the church. Their congregation had virtually doubled overnight. The flow of visitors continued through the summer and even if the church was not experiencing real growth, neither did the enlarged congregation add to the pastoral load!

GROWTH BEGINS

It is one thing to produce a more attractive environment for new worshippers to come to, but quite another to see them actually come. At this point John was able to take advantage of the longevity of the congregation's existence. Even though only forty or fifty people actually attended the church on a Sunday, the number of people on the church membership roll, and those connected with the church through family and friends, was considerably greater. This network of relationships provided a fertile evangelistic territory for someone with John's gift of communication. From the point of view of this wider constituency, John was a young minister with an attractive and laid-back personality. At the very least, this provided a curiosity factor.

As these encouraging developments were beginning, a number of key conversions of individuals who were themselves highly creative people took place. Although in one sense it can be invidious to select some examples and not others, four of these conversion stories help to illustrate something of what was happening more widely in the situation.

Philip had been brought up in the Skipton area. His family

were in farming and Philip had developed a successful business related to the tourist industry. His wife's family were Baptists, and when they moved to Skipton from York they joined the Skipton Baptist Church. There had been a constant Christian witness to Philip through this family connection but the events which acted as a direct catalyst to draw him to a personal Christian commitment took place outside of Skipton itself.

Philip was naturally pleased with his business success. On one occasion his business took him to London, which was not only the business capital of Britain but at a symbolic level epitomised the success-orientated materialist ideology that Philip then espoused. As he left his meeting to return to the train station, he hailed a cab. A few moments later, the cabbie became embroiled in a dispute with the driver of a BMW, which escalated into a street brawl as the two drivers exchanged punches on the pavement. A somewhat shaken Philip left the cab and headed for his train on his own, thinking to himself 'There must be more to life than this.'

Once on the train another traveller, seeing his distress, asked him what the problem was. His travelling companion turned out to be a city banker and a Christian. He explained to Philip the need to be born again. It was easily possible for Philip to dismiss such talk. Once safe in the comfort of his own BMW, driving from the station to his home, he turned on the radio for some company. The programme was *Pick of the Week*; one of the extracts that it featured was an actor reading one of George Whitefield's sermons. The sermon was on the subject, 'You must be born again'. That was enough for Philip. Before he reached Skipton, he had stopped his car and made a decision to become a Christian.

Philip's baptism was an unusual event. In the first place he wanted to be baptised in his business suit to signify his intent to place all that he was and all that he had at the disposal of the Lord he now served. Secondly, he had invited a large number of people to come, including all his employees and their families. Brian and Diane were the parents of one of his employees and they were so surprised by the whole idea of what was going to happen that even though they normally never attended a church, they decided to go. They were impressed by what they saw and heard. Later, when Diane was ill, John Lewis went to visit. On his arrival at the sickbed he found that Diane had been drawing. The subject of her sketch was Christ on the cross. The very act of drawing this picture had caused her to so identify with the person on the cross that she found herself wanting to make a Christian commitment.

Diane was on anti-depressants at that time and was able, with prayer, to gradually come off the drugs that she was using. Later, she felt that she might be able to help others who were dependent on anti-depressants, so she formed a small self-help group. Some twenty-five people are now in the group, five of whom have also become Christians. The medical and social service professions have co-operated and have been surprised and delighted at the effectiveness of this programme.

Another church member was very concerned for her son, Stephen, who in his teens had apparently rejected his family in favour of the local drug-orientated counter culture. The church had prayed regularly for this young man and his partner, though neither of them had much contact with their family and still less contact with any church.

John Lewis had a direct contact with Stephen's partner while ministering to her following the death of her father in a tragic farming accident. Shortly after this event, she was in hospital having a baby. John visited her in the hospital and found her asking to become a Christian. He felt that this was a little soon, as she knew little of the implications of becoming a Christian, and so he left her some literature to read. After he left, a Christian nurse seeing what she was reading spoke to her, and led her to make a commitment to Christ.

In the meantime, Stephen was beginning to think. He was aware of changes in his partner as a result of her becoming a Christian. The birth of their child also had an impact on him. Late one night while returning from Leeds, having gone there to collect some drugs which he used to supply, in the middle of a violent storm in a field he committed his life to Christ.

He wanted others to know of his commitment to Christ and

he told his story to the local press who gave it prominent coverage. Such a story made a significant impact in so relatively small a community as Skipton.

Another entrepreneur in the Skipton area had started attending the Baptist church with his wife, but had largely rejected the Christian faith as being discredited from an intellectual point of view. At that time, John Lewis had been influenced by the reasoned apologetic for the Christian faith that he had encountered through one of the speakers at the annual Evangelist's Conference held at Swanwick. He began to speak to the man about some of these issues, and without realising it, happened to hit on the one issue that the entrepreneur knew a great deal about—it was the area of his post-graduate scientific research. For this man, the conversation with John represented the first time that he had felt any sense of intellectual challenge in relation to the Christian faith. He did not have a sudden conversion experience, but he was able to make his way more slowly towards a Christian experience because he had become aware that faith did make sense after all.

A CLIMATE FOR THE UNCHURCHED

The effect of so many new Christians coming into the church from an unchurched background helped in itself to create a welcoming environment for other unchurched people. However, John Lewis was not content to leave such a climate to develop by itself. He was also working hard to assist the process.

His awareness of the need for change in this area was reinforced by one incident in particular. During a period of outreach to the local schools, he realised that very few of the children had any experience of attending church. He therefore issued an invitation to any children who did not already attend a church, to come with their parents on the next Sunday. To his partial surprise, thirty-nine children turned up the following week, many with their parents. Some came early and were already there when he opened the door. One of the ladies asked him, 'Do I pay to get in now?' The question slightly shocked him, but it also helped him to see that the church was not really ready for the unchurched, especially for those from a non-book culture. That experience also reminded him that the level of potential receptivity to the gospel among the unchurched is often higher than those inside the church sometimes suppose it to be.

John has worked hard to improve the 'user-friendliness' of the church in at least four key areas.

1. He has attempted to improve the public profile of the church. We have already referred to the attractive leaflet that he used for visitors. He has extended this philosophy to everything that the church produces. Even his business card conveys good design. A hanging sign, rather like a swinging pub sign, using wrought iron and a colour scheme with lettering that reflects the nearby conservation area, gives a feeling that these people know what they are doing. The church has an office and a family centre (which replaced the old school room), both of which are clearly signposted. They help to give a contemporary feel to the church.

2. The outreach efforts of the church are attractive and imaginative. One evangelistic initiative involved the production of a thoroughly professional newspaper, which was delivered to 14,000 homes in Skipton and the surrounding villages. The local media is utilised whenever possible. John writes a regular column for the local paper. His approach to events is highly innovative. Whereas other churches have 'men's prayer breakfasts', Skipton Baptist Church has a 'high cholesterol fellowship'! The quality of other events is enhanced by the fact that they are held in a high-quality hotel, owned by a family one of whom attends the church regularly. The design of the invitations and the communication skills of the speakers all serve to convey a sense of excellence.

3. Considerable change has taken place in the programmes that the church offers. The Sunday School area is perhaps the easiest area to see the kind of changes that have been needed, to attract children of all backgrounds, whether from churched or unchurched families. With the help of some very imagina-

tive teachers, Sunday School has become the Sunday Gang. Teaching has taken on a strong activity orientation, the main point of which has been to attempt to make the experience as much fun for the kids as possible. At the same time they attempt to create an environment in which youngsters are able to make a decision for Christ and experience something of what it means to follow him. John is aware that some of these kids might drift from the church in their mid-teens; but at the very least, he is concerned that they should have positive memories of what took place when they were present.

4. Changes to the worship services have happened more slowly. There is a strong focus on the message time which is usually around thirty minutes long. The messages that are preached are strongly related to contemporary issues; in that sense they closely resemble the approach to preaching adopted by Willow Creek. There is a strong sense of fun in the service, with imaginative presentations for the young people and children, often given in the form of a children's message before the children leave for their own activities. Contemporary music has made an appearance and although as yet there is no regular drama ingredient, services feel relaxed and friendly to those who come for the first time. Some multi-media presentations take place on special occasions.

AN AWARENESS OF WILLOW CREEK

Most of the changes listed above were introduced largely because John's own awareness of what was needed to reach the unchurched told him that these were good and necessary developments. However he did begin to receive some stimulation from the other side of the Atlantic when one of his church members visited a large church in Florida (First Baptist Church in Orlando) in 1987. He urged John to visit the States, which he did. He immediately noticed how those who were growth leaders were affirmed in American church life. He noticed also how it was possible for business people and those who were successful in life to feel part of the church in America. He felt that by contrast the church in Britain too often seems to have little to say to those who are successful in life, as if the gospel is only for those who are 'down and out'.

By 1990 he was obtaining inspiration from the preaching of the American minister Chuck Swindoll. He felt that Swindoll's preaching style was helpful in relating the Christian message to contemporary life situations. He also began to hear about Willow Creek. He ordered as many tapes and other literature on the church as he could. As he listened to those messages, chiefly the ones that came from the leader's conferences, he began to say 'We're already doing that.' This contact helped to reassure him that he was on the right track. In particular, he was struck by how similar his core values were to those of Willow Creek. The material from that source helped to strengthen many of his existing convictions, and to further sharpen the direction that he was attempting to take.

More recently, the inspiration of Willow Creek was reinforced when John heard three of the staff members from that church—Lee Strobel, Jerry Butler and Mark Middleberg—give a presentation at the Baptist 'Mainstream' conference in January 1992. That contact led to him attending a leader's conference at Willow Creek in February 1992.

FUTURE HORIZONS

At this time, the original attendance of forty to fifty people that greeted John Lewis when he arrived in 1986 has grown to a regular congregation of up to 250 in the morning and a smaller group of 60 in the evening service. Nearly all of the original group has stayed as the church has grown, although there was some opposition. On one Sunday morning, the congregation was greeted by a member who handed out leaflets to those entering worship, protesting about the developments that were taking place. Such picketing has been unusual!

The congregation is drawn mostly from Skipton itself, though a number of people do come from the outlying villages and a very few travel up to thirty miles to attend. Some other churches in the area have heard of the growth and some visitors come to see what they can learn. The present congregation has a good mix of ages and socio-economic groups, and as such is highly representative of Skipton as a community. Older people seem to enjoy the services. A good number invite their friends. John relates that the reaction of many older people is to say something like 'When we used to go to church as children we had to sit up straight and keep quiet. It's lovely to see how the church has changed and become so friendly.'

In Church Growth terms, the congregation reached capacity some time ago. The building only seats 250 without extra chairs being used. It is possible to add a small amount of extra seating capacity and that will take place in the near future. After that, the only real method of adding extra space will be to move from one morning service to two.

John is helped in his ministry by the activities of his wife and another member of the congregation both of whom are gifted in the area of pastoral work. There are a number of people who are both committed and creative in a whole range of ministries, even in the area of song writing, who greatly add to the sense of team ministry. Other able assistants help him with secretarial and other administrative tasks. The provision of this unpaid assistance has meant that the team has been able to grow without any salary cost to the church. That almost certainly will not be possible in the future. It is already clear that the addition of a staff member to further develop the youth and children's work would prove very valuable indeed.

I have to admit that I was a little surprised by all that I saw taking place in Skipton Baptist Church simply because, viewed from one perspective, it all seems so unremarkable as a congregation. While it is true that there is a contemporary feel to the ministry that takes place, and while that ministry has struck a chord with a number of people who were previously unchurched, the base for all this has been a very traditional church. Despite the new décor which has given a very pleasant feel to the facilities—especially to the family centre—many aspects of the church look and feel traditional. However, it is important to understand that in a community such as Skipton this blend of the new and the traditional has been an important element in building confidence in what was happening.

During the same period that John Lewis has been exercising his ministry in Skipton, a group from one of the house church networks began a congregation in the town. It did not succeed and has since closed. One wonders if it had too much that was new and not enough that was traditional. We need to be aware that whereas most churches that seek to reach the unchurched, especially in larger cities, will gain some advantage by starting from scratch with a new congregation, that may not be true of smaller towns. Skipton Baptist Church helps to remind us that the task of reaching the unchurched will require some models of 'doing church' that have a good mixture of old and new.

CHAPTER TWELVE

Bridging the Gap

S WINDON CHRISTIAN FELLOWSHIP was concerned by the number of totally unreached young people in the town. They were aware that many were not fitting into conventional church structures. Towards the end of the 1980s there came a conviction that it might be time to try a slightly different approach. The opportunity for a fresh approach came with the decision to hold a town-wide mission among teenagers in October 1990.

The mission on 'Livebeat 90', centred around the group Heartbeat and the director of New Generation Ministries, Ray Goudie. The event lasted for four nights and was held in a big top in the middle of the town. Ray Goudie had for some time been a key voice in the nation regarding a change in attitudes to youth outreach and follow up. John Gibson, the leader of Swindon Christian Fellowship, worked closely with Ray in the early plans for the mission and so from the inception of the planning there was a desire to look beyond the immediate event to a longer term strategy. A key ingredient in the strategy was the inclusion of a Christian rock group '65 dba' who were committed to working for a year–September 1990 to the end of August 1991–on the project.

The group and the other workers were to spend September

and some of October building towards the mission as a focal point. But the intention of the mission would not be primarily to seek decisions for Christ from those that attended, so much as to encourage them to attend a five-week follow-up event that would seek to explain the Christian faith over a longer period of time. The hope was that this follow-up event would help to bridge the gap between the excitement of the mission itself and an ongoing committed discipleship on the part of any who did want to become Christians. In view of its aim, the follow-up event was to be called 'The Gap'.

Approximately 120 youngsters attended the first sessions of 'The Gap' immediately following the mission. Before long it became clear that what had been intended as a follow-up event had struck a chord with those that attended. The Gap had come to stay for significantly longer than five weeks.

CHANGE THE ONLY CERTAINTY

Having made the decision that the project should last longer than five weeks, The Gap moved into a second phase which lasted approximately four months. During this time, the group of young people who had been attracted by the mission were also bringing their friends to The Gap. This initial period was therefore strongly evangelistic, with large numbers of young people both coming and going. As the high turnover of young people began to settle down, the activity tended to centre more on a discipling emphasis, so that by the end of this period a more solid and stable group of converts had been established.

The next phase was marked by a move to a night-club venue in the centre of Swindon. This change of venue brought a fresh set of problems for those who were leading the venture. Difficult issues would need to be considered while they were meeting in this new location. It was also true that the venue brought a degree of 'street cred' for those who attended. Early problems with maintaining discipline were eased by the employment of a professional bouncer on the door who was able to keep out those who had earlier been thrown out.

However, the night-club venue included some significant

drawbacks, not the least of which was that there was a need to charge a £1 entry fee. The young people had never been charged for entry to the mission or The Gap. Increasingly, those who were running The Gap felt that there was a need to reassess the direction of the project. That need was reinforced by the awareness that the commitment of 65 dba finished at the end of August. Those involved in the group would be moving on to other projects.

There followed a time which those who were working closely with the project regarded as a death experience. The leaders announced that The Gap would be closing down. For those who were interested, there would be a prayer meeting, the purpose of which would be to seek God's guidance as to what He wanted to do amongst young people in the town. For those who were leading The Gap, a key question had always been 'How many youngsters have been attracted by the music and the lights and how many have really had a genuine experience of God?'

The death of The Gap and the start of a prayer meeting brought a clear answer to this question. To the surprise of the leadership some forty young people came regularly, simply to pray. God used the prayer meeting as a core group for the resurrection of The Gap in the September of 1991.

THE TEAM

Although the mission, Livebeat '90, had been initiated and facilitated by Swindon Christian Fellowship, the driving force for much of what happened in The Gap depended on input from three churches. All three churches could be described as 'house church' in their origins. Remarkably, all three belonged to very different networks. The reason for the strong involvement of these three groups in particular related to their high level of commitment to evangelism among young people in general and to schools work in particular. The original team leader for The Gap was John Gibson. Swindon Christian Fellowship committed a part-time worker to the project. Croft Christian Fellowship also supported a full-time youth worker and probably had the largest existing group of young people of any of the three churches that were co-operating in the project. Highworth Community Church, the third of the three churches, employed a schools worker; Greg Thorne. Although their base was on the outskirts of Swindon, they had, through Greg's work, been investing in young people throughout Swindon for some time.

The change in the format of The Gap, together with the departure of some of the original music group, meant a significant realignment within the leadership team. Greg Thorne of Highworth Community Church, together with his wife Helen became the co-leaders of the new team. Chip Bailey of Croft Fellowship and Richard Gibson, Gill Food and Simon Halls of Swindon Christian Fellowship make up the rest of the core team of leaders. The leadership group is further reinforced by a number of volunteer helpers.

For the purposes of this brief study, I have not looked in any detail at the means by which each of the leaders involved in The Gap became Christians themselves. Greg Thorne, who is the present co-leader with his wife Helen, was not brought up as a Christian and did not become a Christian until the age of twenty. Although he was influenced both by the death of his father and by his mother's decision to become a Christian a few years earlier, the actual process which led directly to his becoming a Christian centred on the Gerald Coates evangelistic event 'The Banquet'. It could be argued that many of the ingredients of The Banquet are not unlike some of the key elements in The Gap. The eight years following Greg's conversion have included three years with the evangelistic Horizons team and four years as a youth worker employed by Highworth Community Church.

THE CURRENT FORMAT

When The Gap was relaunched in September 1991 the core group of forty who had stayed through the prayer-group phase returned. The opening event was a farewell concert for the band, who were leaving for other projects. Since that time

there has come a gradual growth in the regular weekly attendance—a growth which was greatly aided by the impact of a
second week of mission in February 1992. During this second
mission, events were held in seven schools over a five-day
period, culminating in a concert held in a local college. Some
450 youngsters attended this event with up to 100 being turned
away for lack of space. Around 50 young people made a
commitment to become Christians during this week. The fact
that The Gap already existed in a stable form with an existing
core group was a great help in assisting the follow up to the
mission.

A typical attendance at the Tuesday evening Gap following
the mission in February has been between eighty and ninety.
This doesn't mean that the same people always come every
week. Greg Thorne estimates that perhaps as many as 120
come at least once in the course of a month. The core group
numbers at least thirty and these tend to meet on a Sunday
evening for prayer and discipleship training.

What does Tuesday evening at The Gap look and feel like?
Try if you can to imagine a mixture of Tiswas, Vic Reeves Big
Night Out and a Scripture Union Beach Mission. The room in
which they meet could hardly hold many more than ninety
people. Music, videos and coloured lights greet those who
enter early in the evening. As events get underway, a band
plays Christian worship songs and a good number of the
youngsters present join in fairly enthusiastically. The music
stops and a number of competitions take place. A short drama
presented by the youngsters themselves (and not by the
leaders), follows. Other ingredients include a time of testimony such as interviewing a new Christian and then a teaching
time when the theme for that evening is presented. Imaginative visual aids are often in evidence. This is not a watered-
down version of Christianity, simply made palatable and easy
to consume for those who don't really care to dine at the table
of the faithful and so have to be persuaded. Rather, this is
hard-hitting and uncompromising in content; but the cultural
clothes are relevant for those who attend, both visually and in
terms of the decibel level. In fact the name of the original

group that stayed for the first year—65 dba—refers to the maximum number of decibels that they were allowed in the big top!

The team meets all day on Tuesdays to pray and to plan the programme both for the Tuesday evening coming and for succeeding weeks. Julie Gibbon, Rosie Bailey and Helen Thorne are involved in prayer for the project, which the whole team regards as critically important. Friday morning is set aside each week to pray. Although there is no formal pastoral structure for regulars at The Gap, Julie and Rosie, together with Jill Food, act as counsellors for the young people.

Despite the strength of the leadership team the goal of the team is to encourage the youngsters themselves to discover their own gifts and ministries. The team is strongly committed to developing the leadership gifts of the youngsters themselves and to working in such a way that The Gap is perceived to be their own project. The Sunday evening sessions are important in terms of the training process which enables this degree of ownership to take place.

There is no formal process for working with newcomers and bringing them through to a Christian commitment. Relationships are the key ingredient. Those who enjoy what takes place come back; over a period of time, friendships are built. Often it is the young people who help their friends to make a commitment. Recruitment to the various events also takes place on the basis of natural friendships, with youngsters bringing their friends.

Is The Gap on its way to becoming a church? So far the evidence would suggest that this is not happening. Although the project targets anyone at secondary school, it is fifteen and sixteen year olds who are the most strongly represented. It is interesting that this is so, since this is precisely the age group which begins to disappear from church life even when those same young people have been regular attenders until then. At this stage, it does not appear that the nucleus of the group is intending to grow old with the project. A number at the older end of The Gap have opted out, on the basis that they are now too old for what is taking place. Many of them have found their way into a variety of local churches. At the same time there seems to have been an intake at the lower end of the age range, thus enabling the group to remain constant in overall age balance. It is probably too early to say whether this process will continue indefinitely.

Is The Gap a means of entertaining the young people from local churches? Certainly, some of the youngsters who attend are from families who attend local churches. However, it would be difficult to argue that this applies to all or even to most of those who attend The Gap. Even if it were true, such an observation would hardly nullify the value of the project. If all that The Gap achieved was to help Christian young people bridge the gap, not between the outside world and church, but the gap between those difficult years of thirteen to twenty, when peer-group pressures are considerably more important than any other influences, then that in itself would represent no small achievement.

There is considerable evidence to suggest that significant numbers of young people from outside the church are being reached. Interestingly, even at the middle end of the age range a good number do find their way to local churches, partly because some of their friends have connections there and they go to be with them. Usually this means Sunday morning worship. A number of those who have made commitments and who might be inclined to come both on a Tuesday and a Sunday evening do not as yet go elsewhere. For this small number of youngsters The Gap is functioning as their church, although this may turn out to be a temporary phenomenon.

PRESENT PROGRESS

Clearly it is very early days for The Gap, so it is rather unfair to even attempt to measure progress to date. Nevertheless, there are some important developments that should be noted.

First, it is very moving to see the extent to which young people are developing their own gifts and ministries. They are reaching those in their own peer group for Christ, and I suspect that there are few situations where such a thing happens in that critical mid-teens age range.

Second, there is already some impact on the work in schools. One young person at least has begun a Christian Union in a school where none existed previously. Twenty young people now attend that meeting in the school.

Third, those adult workers who are involved in schools work have reported that there seems to be a change in the spiritual climate for youth work generally in the town. Many would attribute that change to the spiritual impact of the mission and The Gap.

Fourth, there are already signs that the existence of The Gap is encouraging the development of future leaders for the church as a whole. It is very likely that those who go on to hold leadership positions in adult life will have learnt lessons through the creative energy of The Gap which would be almost impossible to learn in a purely academic setting. Moreover, not only may the challenge of The Gap result in the preparation of future leaders, but it is also possible that without the vision-creating potential of The Gap the leadership potential of many of these young people will be directed towards secular employment instead of Christian work.

What might the future hold? Some church leaders have told me that they were once part of a high-energy, dynamically-led Christian youth group, and that when they hear of The Gap they tend to place this project in the same category. I am not sure that such a judgement is entirely fair. As I have indicated, there is already some evidence that the project is not growing older as the original core group gets older. More importantly, the rather different factor in The Gap is the sense of the long-term commitment of a number of key adult team leaders to the project. They do not see themselves as—in effect—doing a curacy with youth until they can move on to better things working with adults. Working with and developing the ministries of a particular age group is their ministry; as time goes on they are becoming more and more skilled at doing it.

I came away from an evening at The Gap impressed not only with the vision of the leaders but also and more especially with the commitment of the youth. However it does need to be said that The Gap represents a huge investment of money and time, even to maintain the staffing at its present level. That clearly would not be possible without the very considerable commitment of the three churches that are the most involved in the project. Not every church would be able to invest in a youth venture to this degree. It is also obvious that a project of this kind is never going to be self-sustaining in terms of the attenders funding the salaries of the team and meeting the other expenses of the project.

So are the results of the project worth the investment of time, energy and finance? If the model that one uses to make an assessment of this kind is purely that of a church planting model, and if one sees this as an attempt to plant a church among a group of people that is significantly unchurched, then of course the traditional answer would be 'no', simply because it can never be a self-sustaining group. However, if one saw it instead as both a permanent evangelistic activity and as a means of helping those young people who are in church to maintain their Christian commitment through the years when there is a huge fall-out in attendance and commitment, then there is a strong argument for its value and success.

Moreover, there remains the possibility of achieving much more than this. The problem for those seeking to reach young people with the gospel is that the message is so culturally alien that it has been dismissed long before it has even been heard. I well remember working with a group of young people and arriving at the point where enough discussion had taken place for there to be no longer any serious objection to the actual message; but they simply could not imagine a scenario where it would be possible for them to become Christians and survive in the jungle of youth culture. We seemed to be asking them not just to become Christians but to leave their own culture behind and to enter a new, alien and (it has to be said) rather unattractive other culture. If enough young people can be reached with a gospel in a setting that produces sufficient 'street cred' for those who attend, then it might be possible to produce a situation where the gospel only has to deal with the offence of the cross and does not become offensive in every other way.

In the past, many co-operative efforts between churches to launch youth projects have failed to get off the ground because of unstated but very real jealousies about who was going to receive the long-term benefit of the converts. The result has too often been that no-one has had the benefit of the converts; there haven't been any, because the projects never started. We have to be realistic and recognise that the missionary task of reaching young people now requires a level of resource and leadership that few churches will be able to produce. Co-operation is not just a useful way of sharing resources, it is more likely to be essential if we are to see anything happen at all in most situations.

The youth work in many churches can only produce a house group. Groups of that size are simply not enough to maintain a vibrant Christian commitment. Would it not be better to risk losing all of our young people to our church if the result were to be that we should see them firmly embedded in the Kingdom? The Gap offers churches a fresh challenge to be generous with everything that we have for the sake of a new beginning with youth.

CHAPTER THIRTEEN

Among the Cathedrals

THE CITY OF BRADFORD has its centre in a valley but a great deal of the city spills out over the surrounding hills. The houses cascade down the hillsides with the best properties at the top and the worst at the very bottom of the hill. I stood with Robin Gamble, the Vicar of St Augustine's, at one end of his parish. The cold wind was blowing a mixture of rain and sleet into every crevice on our faces. The housing at this end of the parish was just as cold and forbidding as the weather. In front of us was a council housing estate which seemed to be a dumping ground for the social services. 'Problem' families lived here: they presented problems not only for the city authorities, but for the gospel too. The fortress-like frontages of the flats graphically illustrate the impenetrable nature of this community in relation to the gospel.

From where we stood we could see three prominent church buildings. One, with a flag fluttering proudly from its tower, was the Anglican cathedral. The second was not quite as old but nevertheless occupied an important place in the religious life of Bradford. It was the largest Roman Catholic church in a city that has a considerable Catholic population; so the church acts as an unofficial 'cathedral'. The last of the trio, and the most recent arrival on the religious scene, is the huge hanger-like construction known as the Abundant Life church, the undisputed mother church of the Harvestime network among the house churches. Not one of these three churches—all important in their own way to a wider community, and all quite different in their Christian tradition—has made any signficant impact on the homes which stand in their shadow. This stark reality illustrates very well the difficulties of reaching those unchurched people in our land who are part of the alienated working classes.

Robin Gamble has written a book, *The Irrelevant Church*, which has come largely out of his experience working in the parish of St Augustine. It centres on the difficult question of the way that the church has become isolated from the lives of ordinary working people. He notes the problems associated with the use of the terms 'upper class', 'middle class' and 'working class', pointing out that all three terms are huge generalisations. He notes also that Christians are often unhappy about categorising people into 'classes'. But despite these objections the fact remains that there are very large numbers of people in urban areas who do not attend any church at all, and who describe themselves as working-class people.

St Augustine's is clearly set in an urban parish, where the normal experience of the church in general and of the Anglican church in particular is one of decline and closure. Robin Gamble arrived in the October of 1983 to become the vicar of a parish which was facing a bleak future.

At the time St. Augustine's was on the point of closure. It was a huge Victorian barn built to seat 1,100 people, with a small but very committed congregation. Everything that could go wrong with a building had gone wrong with St. Augustine's: wet rot, freezing temperatures and a leaking roof which meant that on rainy days there were more buckets than people in church.[1]

At one level, Robin felt that things were so bad that he

could hardly fail, since no-one really expected great success to come in a situation like this. However, it was hardly in his nature to think in such terms. Robin wanted the church to grow. The problem was knowing where to start.

BRADFORD BORN AND BRADFORD BRED

Robin Gamble was born and brought up on a large council housing estate on the other side of Bradford. His father had been an adult convert to Christianity, this pivotal event taking place in his middle years. Before that time he had been a man who had given a great deal of his time and energy to causes such as the Labour Party. Following his conversion that energy went into the church. Robin was the youngest of three children and despite the relative lateness of his father's conversion cannot recall a time when he was not being taken regularly to the local parish church. His was the only family from the estate who attended.

Without wishing to make too much of it, Robin Gamble remembers that he was something of a trial to his parents as a teenager and when he announced that he wanted to train for the ministry the reaction of his parents was a mixture of disbelief, joy and anxiety. His teenage years had been such that his training had to include study for 'A' levels, so it was a longer than usual training period. Two curacies, the second in a very suburban situation in York, gave him a much wider experience of life. Though he has never lost his working-class roots, he did not feel any necessity to return to a working-class area. On the contrary, it had not been the kind of ministry that he was seeking.

The fact that he had not sought such an experience made it all the more difficult to know where to start in such a parish, but before he finally agreed to come, he had a crucial meeting with the PCC. He does not remember exactly what he said at that meeting, though he does not believe that he made any demands; but he did attempt to make clear the central thrust of his thinking. That included the certainty that he was not coming as a youth worker, though he had a good track record with young people, nor was he coming to begin community programmes. He told them that he would be committed to evangelism and that the services would need to change. His intention was simply to ensure that if they agreed to his coming they would have some idea of who and what they were going to get. He was convinced that whatever else happened it would be vital for the existing church to be united in all that they did.

BEGINNING WITH THE FRINGE

Robin Gamble is familiar with Church Growth thinking. He describes St Augustine's as 'somewhat charismatic' and is familiar with movements such as John Wimber's 'signs and wonders' emphasis. The church has seen undoubted growth. The thirty or so who attended morning worship when he first arrived have now increased to a total of 250 or more. Is there a secret to the growth of the church? Robin Gamble would agree with Peter Wagner's claim that church growth means hard work both for the vicar and the congregation, much more than any secret prescription! He points to what he calls the 'bread and butter' of church life, by which he means worship and welcome. He believes strongly that most churches, and the Anglican church in particular, will grow if they offer a strong sense of worship combined with the right welcome to those who come. This unspectacular strategy has formed the backdrop for much of what has taken place at St Augustine's.

When he and his wife first arrived in the parish, he gave priority to two areas of activity. First, he attempted to make the worship as warm and as welcoming as he possibly could. His conviction was that if he could succeed in that area, a reasonable proportion of those who came would return. Second, he concentrated on evangelism. What form did this take? In *The Irrelevant Church*, he lists the close contacts that most Anglican churches have:

-people who have recently left the church, perhaps during a previous incumbency;

—occasional attenders;
—strangers who simply 'turn up' for odd reasons or no reason;
—friends and family of those already committed;
—people who receive a church magazine or attend the annual Spring Fair or bazaar, etc;
—those who come to us for baptism, weddings, funerals;
—interested parents of Sunday school children, etc.[2]

The strategy was to work with all of those on the above list and then to 'put himself about a bit'[3] all over the parish, whenever and wherever he could, in pubs, working men's clubs, schools and community functions. He wanted to be sure that people knew him and recognized him. The intention was not to enter some kind of popularity stakes, but rather to ask everybody he met, 'Are you ready to hear something more of God?' In short, he was concerned to make as many contacts as possible in order to seek the receptive. The priority was to make some adult converts.

When I first came to St. Augustine's there were people who expected me to launch all sorts of programmes, but I had to push these expectations to one side and be single minded. It was crucial that we set out to produce first and foremost about twenty adult converts. Once the church began to grow numerically the whole morale of the congregation increased. We became stronger qualitatively and quantitively and then, only then, could we begin to diversify and slowly develop other programmes.[4]

This strategy produced a slow, gradual and constant growth. Over the first four years, the thirty souls that had been there before Robin's arrival became some eighty in the morning and forty in the evening (some of whom were 'twicers' and others of whom had not attended the morning service). At this point, and only at this point, it became possible to knock down the old building and replace it with a new structure tied in imaginatively to parts of the previous structure. The period of exile while the new building was erected took them to a community centre called North Wing. Growth continued during this time much as before. Received wisdom declares that the completion of a new or refurbished building produces a period of dramatic growth. This did not happen for St Augustine's; the same solid and gradual growth simply continued. However, if the building did not bring dramatic new growth, it did at least provide a base from which to plan different kinds of growth.

THE CENTRE TEAM

The original parish had consisted of very densely packed housing giving a total population of some 20,000 people. Redevelopment took this total down to a figure nearer to 7,000. Some new building, together with the addition to the parish of the area in which we stood to see the three 'cathedrals', has pushed the population back up to around 10,000 people. These changes in boundary, together with the opportunities presented by the new building, were important in terms of the team that has developed around Robin.

The growth of the congregation, which means that St Augustine's is now large compared with other Anglican churches in Bradford, has persuaded the Diocese to assign a curate to the parish. The community centre known as North Wing, which the church used while their building was being prepared, is located in the poorest part of the parish. The church has been able to retain its use and has had a community worker, half-funded by the Church Urban Fund, located there. The church now employs a parish worker who spends half her time on the pastoral work and half at the North Wing Centre. They also employ a part-time secretary/administrator and two full-time people to staff the permanent coffee bar and restaurant which is now a feature of the new church centre.

The team meets together for prayer every week day morning at 8.45 am. Robin has separate meetings with the various team members to discuss the different aspects of the work of the church. In addition to these paid workers, a number of other highly committed and talented workers contribute to a people resource which scarcely existed when Robin arrived in 1983.

The new facility would be very much less useful without the human resource that makes it work but equally it has provided a valuable context within which the team works. Robin recalls that when the new building was being considered, the Diocese requested that there should be a competition between a number of plans.

The various plans were submitted to the PCC for their consideration. Robin had a very clear personal preference but he was also fairly sure that it would not be the one that was approved; of all the plans, it looked the least like a church building. However, because he was so committed to the idea of the church moving forward unitedly, he felt that it would not be wise to comment at all on any of the plans. To his pleasure and surprise the plans that the church chose were the ones that he would have chosen himself.

It was certainly an unusual choice but one very suited to their later goal of attempting to reach those beyond the fringe, the completely unchurched in the parish. Entering the bright blue and yellow metal doors of the church centre it feels very much as if you are entering a local authority leisure centre. That sense of familiarity is reinforced in the interior of the church. The large foyer consists of an open-plan restaurant and coffee bar area. The large servery gives a warm and obvious welcome which is somehow much more comforting than a more formal 'enquiries' desk. The food smells and tastes good and is offered at exceptionally low prices. I can strongly recommend the bacon rolls!

The foyer has a glass and wood screen that allows visual access to the very pleasant, light and airy, multi-purpose worship area. A gallery provides a further multi-purpose lounge and meeting space which in turn leads on to the church office. Downstairs, the local authority operates a small library which uses both a small room and, by using mobile book displays, is able to overflow into the foyer. The centre looks and feels busy and active all through the week, with a constant stream of people coming and going for a variety of purposes. This is the helpful context for an attempt to present church for the unchurched working classes who lie beyond the normal fringe of the church's life.

SUNDAY SPECIAL

How do you present church for the unchurched in an urban as compared to a city-centre or suburban setting? St Augustine's answered this question by launching something called 'Sunday Special' as a kind of church plant within the same congregation. It might help to understand the context for the launch of Sunday Special by describing the feel of the other services that take place. The regular pattern consists of a 9.30 am Sunday morning service that currently attracts about 110 people, most of whom are adults. This is an informal, mildly charismatic service which also has some traditional feel to it. The evening 6.30 pm service is a much more informal and lively service with a higher percentage of young people in attendance. There is more emphasis on teaching and worship of a charismatic nature. Robin believes that some 60 to 70 per cent of the 135-150 strong evening congregation have not attended an earlier service. it is important to note that there is also a rather more traditional mid-week communion service which keeps closely to the words of the liturgy and generally only uses more traditional hymns.

Sunday Special approximates to a more 'family service' format, but is emphatically not referred to as a family service. It was launched on Mother's Day in 1991 and so is at the time of writing just over a year old. The service features competitions, lively music, colour, noise, and testimony. There is generally a ten- to fifteen-minute talk, which picks up on the theme of the service. The themes usually last for a few weeks at a time with each week featuring a different aspect of the overall theme. A recent example was 'Bart Simpson meets Jesus'. Each week featured a different character from the cartoon series meeting Jesus. Large colourful cartoon posters were displayed at the front of the church. Part of the intention of the themes is to act as attention-getters for those outside the church and to generate as much publicity as possible. The Bart Simpson theme was imaginative enough to attract the attention of the local press.

At this time, some fifty to sixty adults and children, as well as a few that stay over from the earlier service, attend the Sunday Special service. The launch can be judged to have been a success and there is now an attempt to stabilise the event; there is an awareness that one of the features of the unchurched people who come is that until their commitment is more established, they tend to blow 'hot and cold'. The next move is to ask six families who have come to the church through this service to take a large measure of responsibility for the planning of the event. This is a conscious attempt to develop a sense of ownership for the event from people who are best-equipped to understand the mind-set of the unchurched.

When the Sunday Special was first launched it was accompanied by as much publicity as the church could generate; it took the form of leaflets, posters and press articles. Indeed, according to Robin Gamble, some people might be likely to comment that St Augustine's is never out of the local press! However, despite all this publicity, Robin Gamble is convinced that personal invitation remains the single most important factor in actually persuading people to come. 'I am a bit obsessed with this,' he says. The publicity tends to create a backdrop of interest and receptivity which helps to provide an opportunity for a personal invitation. Robin acknowledges that still only a minority of people actually invite others, but they continue to work at training people to give invitations. He is convinced that such training involves the instilling of a certain degree of habit or discipline. Using his own case as an illustration, he acknowledges that he is something of a natural evangelist, but that he works hard to become a better evangelist. He maintains that everyone can make some improvement in their invitational skills given practice, time and discipline.

Gradually those who have been genuinely unchurched have been coming to the Sunday Special service. But once someone has attended a service, what comes next? Normally, once someone has attended two or three times, one of the staff members will visit and attempt to make an assessment of how they can help that person move forward in their understanding of the faith. In other words, there is a concern to offer a way forward which is in a sense 'tailor-made' for that person or family. It may be that the best way forward is just to continue to visit and build friendships. Other available options would include the offer of a 'Good News Down Your Street'[5] type of faith-sharing team to come and lead studies in that person's home. Alternatively they might be invited to attend a small group that is studying a 'Christian Basics' course. Another option would be to ask someone to give some practical assistance to one or other of the church and/or community projects. Some might be invited to one of the many social functions that the church holds regularly. One such event was the launch of Robin Gamble's book, *The Irrelevant Church*. St Augustine's hired a local working men's club for the launch and laid on a good meal. Tony Collins, the publisher of the book, travelled from the rural idyll of Kent for the event and cannot remember ever having been at a book launch that looked anything like it.

Despite the fact that there is no set route, the importance of a consistent and regular follow up for those who begin to attend is clear.

A MISSION STRATEGY

As St Augustine's has developed, a three-pronged mission strategy seems to have evolved. The first ingredient is still that which Robin Gamble began with: evangelism. As he expresses it in his book:

> It is essential that this new beginning be based on evangelistic effectiveness, for two reasons. Firstly, the poor have been denied Jesus for too long. To give someone Jesus is to give them the best and most valuable part of creation's life. Put crudely, the working classes have never had their fair

share of God.... Secondly, the church nationally is haemo-
rrhaging. We are losing members at an alarming rate. We
are reaching the point where we just do not have the members to carry out any sort of effective mission, be it social or
spiritual.[6]

The second prong is that of a social caring ministry. St
Augustine's operates a substantial food pantry and in a parish
where there is substantial poverty they help to feed a surprisingly high number of people in the course of a week. As we
indicated, a coffee bar and restaurant is in operation five days a
week. The food is sold very cheaply, and a 'pensioners' special'
is offered at lunch time.

The project at North Wing has become a substantial community centre venture, with all kinds of groups operating from
the facilities there. Many, though not all, of the groups that
use the premises are staffed by St Augustine's. A whole range
of community activities operate both from the North Wing
centre and from the main church centre. These include pensioners' groups, children's work (especially in the summer),
one-parent family support groups, a clothing store, help with
the transport of furniture, and a loan scheme (which is about
to become a credit union).

A more recent venture has been to introduce a group called
Christian listeners. As their name suggests, their function is to
provide a listening ear to those who are distressed, are lonely
or who simply need to talk to someone. They do not seek to
counsel or advise but just to listen. At the moment, this service
is not heavily advertised in the community, but there is a link
with the local doctor's surgery which provides referrals.

The third prong of their mission strategy is what Robin
Gamble calls their 'prophetic work'. In this category they
become involved in campaigning activities beyond simply
offering practical help to those in need. The intention is to
seek to provide a Christian voice in areas of society where the
church believes that change is needed. A recent example
would be their involvement in the group, 'Christians against
the poll tax'.

These three parts to their mission strategy has given St Augustine's a platform and a voice which allows them to be heard, not only by the fringe members of the Christian church but by those who would normally never darken the doors of any church, no matter how lively it might be. There is an increasing feeling that the Sunday Special service is not just a token attempt to reach out a little, but is only the first step in a serious attempt to penetrate those parts of society which have been for so long alienated from the church.

The next concrete step is to launch yet another worship service, but this time to seek to penetrate the most difficult and neglected part of the parish, the area of housing immediately around the North Wing community centre. At this stage, the plan is to use the North Wing centre as the basis for the new venture. There is a feeling that the centre is presently too run-down physically and that the first move will be to refurbish it prior to the launch of a regular worship service there. The intention at this stage is to hold a mid-week rather than a Sunday service. Robin has a vision for an event that will be significantly different in style from anything else that the church engages in at the moment.

The North Wing church plant probably represents a greater challenge than anything else that the church has attempted so far. It certainly involves taking a step which is both actually and symbolically a move outside the present confines of St Augustine's church building. It represents yet another step in the process of St Augustine's moving from a church which called the faithful, only to find that they did not respond, to a genuinely missionary church which desires to seek the lost. St Augustine was one of the first missionaries to Britain. The parish seems to be appropriately named!

FOOTNOTES

1. Robin Gamble, *The Irrelevant Church* (Monarch: 1991), p 147f.

2. *Ibid*, p 161.

3. Robin Gamble used this phrase in an interview with the author, 15 April 1992.

4. Robin Gamble, *op cit*, p 149.

5. See Michael Wooderson, *Good News Down Your Street* (Grove Books: 1982).

6. Robin Gamble, *op cit*, p 149.

Postscript

T HREE WORDS COME TO MIND when reflecting on Willow Creek and on the various British case histories. First, the word *creativity*. The importance of many of the approaches explored is not that they are entirely original; indeed most if not all of the churches that are described are engaged in the kind of 'bread and butter' ministry that has sustained thousands of churches through the centuries. Offering an invitation to friends, presenting a gospel message, seeking to disciple converts—these are hardly original ideas. But the creativity that has been brought to these somewhat ordinary tasks by people who are very often winsome, lively and attractive individuals is notable. More often than not the creative process has been significantly enhanced, by the ability of the individuals who acted as pioneers to draw other creative people around them in a team relationship.

The second word is *cost*. It is all too easy to look at churches that have grown and perhaps even feel a sense of jealousy. Yes, the people involved in these churches are working hard—but wouldn't we all work hard if we had the stimulation of some of these creative situations? Wouldn't such churches bring out the best in all of us? No doubt that is true, but we tend to forget that the same people who are working now in such encouraging surroundings were paying a tremendous price for growth before anything significant started to happen. Often the creative genesis that allowed a church to see remarkable events take place began with the formation of a set of relationships deeply bonded in the pain of being willing to give anything for the sake of seeing the unchurched come to Christ. Far fewer churches and leaders are willing to pay such a price than we might imagine.

That brings us to the third word, *commitment*. It is not unusual to find creative people working together over a period of time. Probably many of us can remember times in our life when we were part of, or close to, a creative group of people. It is much more unusual to find those creative people willing to pay a price to exercise their creativity not just for a short time but over an extended period. Such willingness requires a single-minded commitment to a cause which will then find its expression in a long-term ministry. Reaching the unchurched happens less as a result of a sudden short-term burst of activity than through a commitment to working out a strategy over a long period of time.

Despite the team participation in many of these situations, it is nevertheless true that the involvement of at least one key individual has been critical in the development of the church or project. Willow Creek is unusual among American megachurches in that very few people identify it first and foremost with an individual. When you mention the name 'Willow Creek', you are more likely to obtain the reaction, 'That's the church with a Seeker Service' than you are to find people responding, 'That's Bill Hybels' church.' The concept is more important than the person. And yet it has to be acknowledged that Willow Creek would hardly be the same place without Bill Hybels.

The contribution of particular individuals is vital to the way in which God seeks to fulfil his mission in the world. When we come to consider how the unchurched might be reached for the kingdom of God in European churches, we must be conscious of the notable absence in the church of the kind of creative people who seem to be only too available in every other sphere of endeavour.

From time to time in the course of my own ministry I meet individuals who were born and educated in Great Britain and emigrated to other English-speaking countries as adults. There in their adopted country, whether New Zealand, Australia, South Africa, or the United States of America, they heard the Christian message, often for the first time, and became Christians themselves. Some of these converts return home. As they attempt to share their new-found faith with their relatives, and in some cases their former friends and workmates, two realities quickly dawn on their consciousness.

First, they realise that if those with whom they share their faith do respond, it will be very difficult for them to find a church in which they will feel comfortable. Certainly there do not seem to be many churches around where men in particular can feel comfortable in the way that they do seem to be able to feel comfortable in overseas churches. Second, they quickly understand, sometimes with awe and other times with sadness, that if they had not emigrated it is almost certain that they would not now be Christians.

The leaders of churches who are reaching the unchurched are unusually gifted people. Often they are gifted leaders and communicators. It is notable how many of those that we studied in the case histories were themselves from an unchurched background. Nearly all occupy a narrow fifteen-year age band, somewhere between 28 and 43. It is encouraging to witness the work of such people but, so far at least, they are few and far between, especially in Europe.

When we look at the history of world mission more widely, it becomes clear that the most successful missionaries have not necessarily been those who have themselves brought large numbers of people to Christ. It is rather that those who have made a significant difference to the mission field have been people who were able to convert and properly disciple a relatively small number of key leaders and opinion-formers in the communities in which they were working. It tended to be those who were part of the indigenous community as leaders that then went on to bring large numbers of people to Christ and so bring a real breakthrough in mission.

As we look at the mission field of Europe, it seems to be the case that we not only see many who are unchurched, but large numbers of people who are part of the long-term unchurched. These millions of people not only have no contact with the church, but contact has been become so distant that they have almost become different people groups. My suspicion is that the creative 'breakthrough' people whom the church needs in order to reach the vast masses of the unchurched in significant numbers have not yet been converted and discipled.

If I am correct in thinking that these key 'breakthrough' people are as yet unreached themselves, then it is much more likely that the relatively small number of churches who are engaging significantly with the unchurched will be the ones who succeed in bringing such 'breakthrough' people to Christ. It may well be that what we are beginning to see in Britain is the construction of long-term mission bases which, in the short term, will not make headlines, but which in the longer term may provide the training schools from which will emerge the missionaries to the unchurched for the coming decades.

British Church Growth Association

The British Church Growth Association was formed in September 1981 by a widely representative group of Christians committed to church growth either as researchers, teachers, practitioners or consultants.

The BCGA aims to help and encourage the church in Britain to move into growth in every dimension. The facilities and resources of the BCGA are available to researchers, consultants, teachers, practitioners and those just setting out in church growth thinking. The Association endeavours to offer practical help as well as encouraging and initiating church growth thinking and research.

Membership of the BCGA is open to both individuals and organisations interested in or involved in the theory or practice of church growth. On payment of an annual subscription members are entitled to receive the *Church Growth Digest* (the journal of the Association) four times a year, information about activities through the Newsletters, special discounts on conferences and books, membership of the Church Growth Book Service, voting rights to elect members to the Council every two years, links with other researchers, teachers, practitioners, and consultants on a regional or national level as well as help or advice on allied matters.

Further information about the Association and membership is available from the Secretary, British Church Growth Association, 3a Newnham Street, Bedford, MK4 2JR, Tel: 0234 327905.